Bludie Harlaw

Bludie Harlaw
Realities, Myths, Ballads

Ian A. Olson

Heir the bludie battel of the Harlaw was fochtine; gret slachter on baith handis, mony alsweil knychtes as utheris nobles war na mair sein.

Father James Dalrymple (1596)

JOHN DONALD

First published in Great Britain in 2014 by
John Donald, an imprint of Birlinn Ltd

West Newington House
10 Newington Road
Edinburgh
EH9 1QS

www.birlinn.co.uk

ISBN: 978 1 906566 76 0

British Library Cataloguing-in-Publication Data
A catalogue record for this book is available on request
from the British Library

Typeset in Warnock by Koinonia, Manchester
Printed and bound in Britain by T. J. International, Padstow, Cornwall

For Elizabeth

Trustworthy accounts of this famous fight there are none. Lowland historian and ballad composer, as well as Highland seanachie, described what they believed must and should have happened.

Clan Donald historians (1896)

Much has been written about that battle, and some of it is pure fiction.

Irvine of Drum historian (1998)

Contents

List of Illustrations

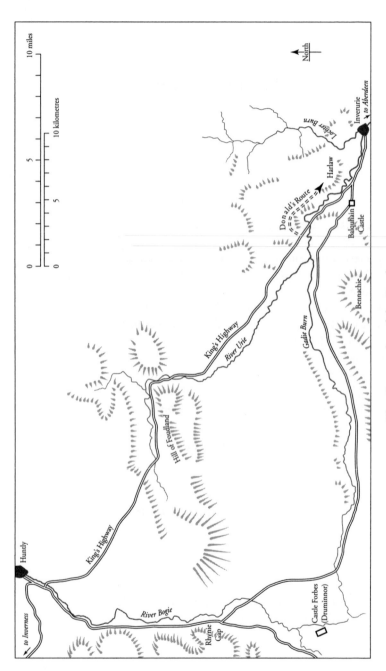

The Geography of the Battle

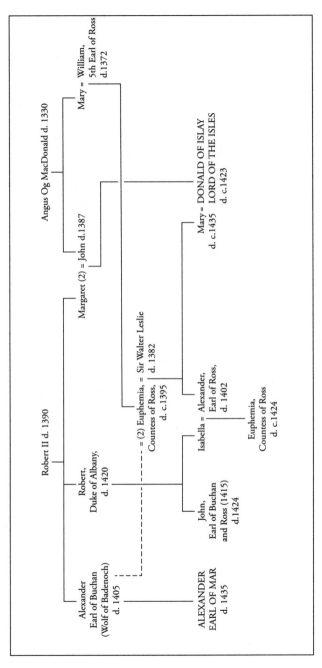

Claims to the Earldom of Ross

1

Introduction

In the summer of 1411, Donald of Islay, Lord of the Isles, invaded mainland Scotland with a huge, battle-hardened army, only to be fought to a bloody standstill on the plateau of Harlaw, fourteen miles from Aberdeen, a town he had threatened to sack. The ferocious battle was described by even hardened mediaeval chroniclers as 'atrocious', with some three thousand dead, dying and wounded on the field.

It should stand as one of the greatest battles ever fought in Scotland, ranking easily alongside Bannockburn or Flodden in size and significance, but it has largely faded now in memory, other than that of Aberdeen, where its 'deliverance' is still celebrated (on the wrong day, because of old and new calendar confusion) at a stark monument commemorating those who fought at 'Red/Reid Harlaw', high on the hill.

Walter Scott dismissed it as having settled for once and for all whether or not 'Celt or Saxon' should rule Scotland, a political comfort perhaps for a Britain still shaken by the memory of the Jacobite Risings of 'wild Scots' from the West.

Written records of Donald's invasion exist in Latin, Scots, Gaelic (only one, alas) and English. Lowland versions tend to dominate, mainly because there had been serious destruction of 'Highland' accounts, especially of the records of the Lords of the Isles themselves. Records also fall into two main groups – a 'first set' written at or around the time, and a 'second set' composed some 300 years later. These later histories tend to be both romantic and highly imaginative, creating noble order where chaos existed before – and form the basis of most popular descriptions of the battle.

There is an unfortunate tendency to view Scottish history as a series of clan battles – Harlaw, especially, being seen as 'Macdonalds versus Stewarts' – which were terminated in the aftermath of the Jacobite

Risings. Thereafter the Highlander morphs into a romantic, even erotic figure, striding the world stage as the hero of Waterloo and suchlike battles, while the Lowlander (curiously clad on occasion in an approximation of 'Highland dress') proceeds with serving a united kingdom.[1] It is during this post-Risings period that the 'second set' of Harlaw histories, many with strong racial connotations, begin to appear.

For over a hundred years serious historians have studied the Lordship of the Isles, the earldoms involved in the battle – Ross, Mar and Buchan – the great families and the Stewart kings of those times, weaving a rich tapestry from the period, a tapestry, like the Bayeux, which evolves over time, reflecting constantly changing allegiances and alliances made and broken as circumstances permitted or encouraged. Geographically it extends from Norway across to the Isles and over to Ireland, from mainland Scotland to England, and even to France, for it is a mistake is to view Donald's invasion, as some do, as a relatively local matter, affecting principally the North-East of Scotland.

From this gratefully acknowledged tapestry I have attempted to draw out the threads of why the greatest magnate in Scotland should have taken an excessive gamble by invading, antagonising and horrifying the mainland Scots, all for – apparently – to make a claim for the Earldom of Ross. The threads are the written records which are presented here both in original form, and with transcriptions and translations.

Two major ballads are included, one probably written around the time and perhaps shedding some light on the conflict, and one fabricated over 350 years later; despite being sung to this day, this latter is of almost no historical value at all. *The Complaynt of Scotland*, published around 1550, depicts a group of shepherds and their wives amusing themselves by singing 'sueit melodious sangis of natural music of the antiquite', one of which was entitled 'the battel of the hayrlau', but the title alone was given.[2] There exist other songs and music carrying the title, 'The Battle of Harlaw', but little is known for certain about them or even the instruments available six hundred years ago.[3] As they may well be of much later composition, commemorating a great past tragedy, as the Scots do so well, I have not included them.

Over the centuries, Highland poets and bards have alluded to the battle, and praised patrons by referring to their ancestors' involvement at Harlaw.[4] With supreme confidence and enthusiasm they have described it as an undoubted victory for Donald.[5] I have thus confined myself to descriptions and arguments given in prose accounts from either side of that conflict.

The early descriptions of the battle were superceded by very much later stories. These accounts, especially the most influential such as Tytler's, have drawn on few, if any, fresh sources, yet they form the firm and confident basis both of 'folk memory' and modern accounts of the conflict, demonstrating the remarkable power of such transformative stories. This has necessitated my recounting the battle and its aftermath several times, in English, Scots and Gaelic, in order to show the differences between the early histories and later accounts as well as those between 'Highland' and 'Lowland' versions. The Latin originals are provided in Appendix I.

It is twenty-five years since I first asked the late David Buchan about his initial research on the Harlaw ballads. I was then beginning to explore the ragged and apparently unreliable interface between such balladry and Scottish history. This was an interest in Scottish history that had been aroused by the then Albany Herald, Sir Iain Moncreiffe of that Ilk, first when a patient of mine, and thereafter as a good friend and guide, a man who combined a remarkable attention to detail with a delight in his subject.

One of the great pleasures in studying Scottish history is the fact that descendants of those who played a part in events such as the Battle of Harlaw are not only still with us, but are more than helpful in the untangling and understanding of the past. Consider, for example, Robert Maitland of Balhalgardy's family – they have farmed the site of Harlaw for over six hundred years; his ancestor 'left the plough to join the battle'.

I am thus grateful for the kind assistance of the following: David Irvine of Drum, Chief of the Name and Arms of Irvine and 26th Baron of Drum; Malcolm Forbes, Master of Forbes; the late James Irvine-Fortescue, 15th Laird of Kingcausie; Sir Lachlan Maclean of Duart and Morvern, 28th Clan Chief; The Very Reverend Allan Maclean of Dochgarroch; James Burnett of Leys, Chief of the Name of Burnett, the late Ian Roderick Macneil of Barra, Chief of Clan MacNeil; the late Douglas Stuart, 20th Earl of Moray. The Master of Forbes entrusted me with his bound manuscripts, 'Memoirs of the House of Forbes', as did the late James Irvine-Fortescue with his family manuscripts, 'The privat historie of the Irvins of Kingcausie'.

The contemporary or near-contemporary Lowland accounts of the battle are largely in Latin and I am indebted to classical scholars Patrick Edwards, Jonathan Foster, and the late Robin Nisbet for their invaluable help with transcriptions and translations.

Although there is a sad dearth of accounts from the 'Highlands' – a term I shall use to encompass both the Highlands and Islands – I have leant heavily on patient Celtic scholars Ronald Black, Colm Ó Baoill and Donald Meek not only for transcription and translation of both Scottish and Irish Gaelic, but also for important historical information.

I am deeply indebted to Caroline Macafee both for her constant support and for her linguistic analysis of the 'Ramsay ballad', the 'Battle of Harlaw', showing it to have been composed not long after the battle.[6]

Aberdeen University Library's holdings are superb in both range and quality; they have been made available to me most ably, especially by Michelle Gait and the ever helpful staff of Special Collections and Archives.

Kenneth Veitch, together with the late Alexander Fenton, edited and published my preliminary exploration, 'The Battle of Harlaw, its Lowland Histories and their Balladry: Historical confirmation or confabulation?', in *The Review of Scottish Culture* in the summer of 2012.[7] He was painstaking with his historical guidance, and as a consequence historians such as Norman Macdougall – 'I feel that everyone interested in the period should read your piece on Harlaw – and learn from it!' – were both generous with their comments and helpful with advice. This in turn encouraged me to attempt this further account of Harlaw from both 'Highland' and 'Lowland' perspectives. Hugh Andrew of Birlinn in particular pressed for a clearer account of how the Lord of the Isles dealt with the reaction to his massive invasion, and the appalling battle it provoked.

Part 1

The Early Histories

Part I

The Early Histories

2

The Opponents: The Lord of the Isles and the Earl of Mar

Donald of Islay, Lord of the Isles

On the plateau of Harlaw, fourteen miles from a vulnerable Aberdeen, stands Donald of Islay, aged about sixty, commander of a huge army of battle-hardened troops, ostensibly there to press his claim to the Earldom of Ross. It is an earldom whose exclaves do in fact extend into the north-east of Scotland, and as far down as Kincardine, so his current positioning has some rationale.[1] But is he simply the headstrong leader of an army of wild men who have ravaged their way from the Isles down to Harlaw in a glorious cattle raid, with the looting of Aberdeen the promised prize, a man greedy for power and land?[2]

He is chief of Clan Donald, Lord of the Isles – in terms of territory and manpower the largest and most powerful province of Scotland – able to raise and command thousands of warriors; his possessions include the Hebridean and inshore islands (with the exception of Skye, an important omission) and territories on the mainland such as Morvern, Garmoran, Lochaber, Kintyre and Knapdale.[3] Clan Donald claim they are descendants of Conn of the Hundred Battles, High King of Ireland, who ruled from Tara, as well as from Colla Uais, a later High King of Ireland, and in the sixth century from Godfrey, son of Fergus Mor, one of the founders of the Scottish kingdom of Dalriada in the sixth century.[4]

From the eighth to the twelfth century, the Isles from Orkney and Shetland down to the Isle of Man and Argyll were under Norse occupation.[5] Settlement and intermarriage with the indigenous Celts produced the *Gall-Gaedhil* ('Foreigner Gaels'), inhabitants of *Innse Gall* ('Isles of the Foreigners').[6] In the middle of the twelfth century, his ancestor Somerled, born probably of a union of a mother from the Dublin Norse and a *Gall-Gaedhil* father, married the daughter of the Norse king of Man and the Isles. Somerled seized control first of Argyll, then Man, and then the remaining Isles.[7] He eventually challenged the Scottish Crown while obtaining the Norwegian title of 'King of the Sudreys' (southern isles), a challenge which led to his defeat and death in 1164. The Clan Donald is named after his grandson Donald, who also combined this challenging the Scottish Crown with friendship with Norway, a policy which in turn his son Angus Mor also followed until the Battle of Largs in 1263 ended Norse overlordship of the Isles.

Angus' son Alexander took an oath of allegiance with England against Bruce, becoming Edward's Admiral of the Western Isles. Captured by Bruce, all his estates were forfeited, but wisely, Alexander's brother Angus Og gave his support to Bruce, both in Bruce's days as a fugitive, as well as at Bannockburn; he was thus rewarded with Isla and Kintyre, Mull, Jura, Coll and Tiree, Glencoe, Morvern and Lochaber.

His son John was an able diplomat who first supported Balliol and England, then David Bruce, and took as his second wife Margaret, daughter of the future Robert II. From this union was born our Donald of Islay, who after his father's death in 1387 became 2nd Lord of the Isles and head of the Clan Donald, although it appears that he had in fact been acting as *de facto* Lord of the Isles from 1376.[8]

Donald's succession was with the consent of his elder half-brother Reginald and the principal men of the Isles.[9] Donald, however, had first to deal with a revolt by his younger brother John, who, being dissatisfied with his meagre inheritance, decamped into Ireland. There he entered the service of Richard II, and established a Macdonald lordship, marrying the heiress of the Seven Glens of Antrim; the brothers later became reconciled.[10]

With the Norse overlordship long gone, the principal chessmen left on the board were now the Lords of the Isles – once again virtually in possession what had been Somerled's realm – as well as the Scottish Crown and the kings of England; each played one against the other with allegiances made and broken as circumstances permitted or encouraged. Donald's father John had sought to retain independence for his Isles' kingdom from a weakened Scottish Crown by entering into treaties with England – treaties which did not prevent John fighting on the side of the French at Poitiers in the Hundred Years War, nor indeed his later submitting to and supporting David II of Scotland in 1369 (as well as marrying his daughter).[11]

Donald's Lordship

This 1369 submission, however, had required John to give his son Donald as hostage in the castle of Dumbarton. Donald was eldest son of John Macdonald's second wife, married with papal dispensation in 1350. Donald's date of birth is not known, but as there were seven siblings born after him, it may fall within the range of 1351 to 1360, making the hostage between nine and eighteen years old. That this did not endear the Scottish Crown to Donald is evidenced by his later attendances at the English court with his brothers, his leagues with both Richard II and twice-renewed defensive alliances with Henry IV.[12]

With the dust of the Wars of Independence settled the Stewart kings were established on the Scottish throne. Although Donald has been taken to be the defender of Celtic independence, a champion in the great death struggle for Scotland between 'Celt and Saxon' or 'Celt and Teuton', in reality he is proud to be a grandson of Robert II and first cousin of Robert III.[13] He holds lands from the Crown and is but one of the great magnates such as the Douglases and the rising Campbells, who also act with considerable freedom in their lordships.[14] He possesses, however, one significant difference – the relationship of the Lordship of the Isles with Ireland, which not only serves as a useful place of refuge but as a great reservoir of experienced fighting men on which he can draw, as this account shows well:[15]

> But Ireland's main role was as an outlet for the surplus military potential of the Lordship. Ever since the thirteenth century mercenary soldiers from this part of Scotland had taken a considerable part in the unceasing strife in that country [Ireland] not only between the English and Irish, but also between rival groupings of Irish kindreds. Many of these mercenaries, termed gall-oglaigh or gallowglasses by the Irish, settled as a more or less permanent military caste in Ireland before 1400, but the annals are witness to the constant traffic across the North Channel throughout the fifteenth century and later. One result of this was that, potentially at any rate, the Lords of the Isles had an enormous reservoir of experienced fighting men on which to

draw. This may explain, in part at least, their ability to put on the field of battle armies which, in terms of numbers and expertise, often matched those at the command of the crown itself . . . which makes less startling the statement that as many as 10,000 men accompanied Donald to Harlaw . . . It is an indication of the military might of the Lordship for much of the fourteenth and fifteenth centuries that almost the only recorded military threat to its borders came from royal armies.[16]

These corps of mail-clad, battleaxe-wielding, heavy infantry were formidable, all fighting on foot regardless of rank, and notorious for being especially effective against mounted opponents.[17] (As will be seen, Walter Bower, a Lowland chronicler mentions the Provost of Aberdeen and burgesses coming out to fight against them at Harlaw. That they would have lasted many minutes against such a foe would seem unlikely).

Robert II's Many Offspring

For Donald, the situation in Scotland was precarious for at least two reasons – firstly the fertility of Robert the Bruce's son, Robert II. This king eventually married his mistress Elizabeth Mure around 1348, thus legitimising their four sons and five daughters. A subsequent marriage to Euphemia de Ross in 1355 produced a further two sons and two surviving daughters, complicating the line of succession. The second reason for concern was Henry IV's continuing imprisonment of the king, James I.

Robert II's many offspring, all had to be provided with titles and land. His first-born, John, Earl of Carrick, had taken the throne as Robert III but retired from active rule, conferring the Dukedom of Albany on his brother. Robert III had two sons, David and James, but David, Duke of Rothesay, died while in Albany's care, and James, aged around twelve, was captured by the English in 1404. As he was to recall poetically after 'twise nine' long years in captivity:

Upon the wawis weltering to and fro,	[waves being tossed]
So unfortunate was us that fremyt day	[unlucky]
That maugré, playnly, quhethir we wold or no,	[in spite of]
With strong hand, by forse, schortly to say,	
Of inymyis taken and led away	

We weren all, and broght in thair contree:
Fortune it schupe non othir wayis to be. [shaped]

James had been captured while being sent to France – away from Albany's 'care' – and was to become James I when his father died that same year. The Duke of Albany, however, who had been acting as Governor of Scotland from 1388, was to make little effort to bring James home for coronation.[18]

Robert II's fourth son, Alexander, Earl of Buchan and Lord of Badenoch, was the 'Wolf of Badenoch', who eventually embarked on a career of rapacity and cruelty, culminating this terrorism with the burning of Elgin Cathedral. A marriage to the Countess of Ross gave Alexander joint control of a vast swathe of Scotland, from Caithness to Fife. Significantly, this included Skye, Lewis and the castle of Dingwall.[19]

Robert II's remaining children gained the Earldoms of Atholl, Strathearn, Menteith, and the Lordship of Lorn. The Wolf's son, the younger Alexander Stewart, obtained the Earldom of Mar in 1405, reputedly by arranging the death of the earl and inviting his widow to marry him. In other words, the Stewart dynasty, or, rather that portion under control of the Duke of Albany, was now severely encroaching upon Donald's realm.[20]

Donald Claims the Earldom of Ross

Donald had the chance to hold back this tide when Euphemia, an apparently ailing child, became the heiress to the Earldom of Ross, for her aunt Margaret, who had a rightful claim to the Earldom, had married Donald.[21] But unfortunately Euphemia's maternal uncle was the Duke of Albany. In 1405 he seized the girl, declared she was his ward, and set about persuading her to enter a nunnery and resign her rights to Albany's son, John, Earl of Buchan.

Donald now claimed the Earldom. In his sixties, this seemed to be his last chance not only to become one of the great earls of Scotland and sit at the royal table, so to speak, but also to secure his realm by gaining control of all Lewis and Skye, as well as the 'buffer state' of Ross.[22] Albany point blank refused his claim and in the summer of 1411 Donald invaded mainland Scotland at the head of a great army.

Suggestions continue to be made that Donald had more on his mind than simply gaining the Earldom of Ross: that he was contending for the throne itself;[23] that he intended to destabilise and frighten the Albany Stewarts by invading the mainland as far south as the Tay;[24] that he was acting in consort with Henry IV and/or with James I, Henry's prisoner.[25]

Best of all, is the concept that Donald was heading a Celtic revival, a return of Somerled, to wrest Scotland from 'the Saxons'. Unfortunately for this fancy, he was going to be opposed by a leader of a Gaelicised military following (with both a Gaelic mother and a fine line in Gaelic poetry) heading an army containing many Gaelic speakers (the language was used as far down as the Tay).[26] Just how 'Celtic' Donald's own people were after four centuries of Norse settlement and intermarriage is also a moot point.[27] He had indeed a good claim to the throne through his wife and the military power to support it, although Douglas and Campbell opposition alone would have been formidable.[28]

Cooperation with England?

Any cooperation with Henry IV can only be guessed at.[29] Although there is a truce in the fighting of the Hundred Years War, it is a war in which Scotland is formally and practically supporting France against England – Donald's father had been captured fighting at Poitiers. Yet, added to war in Wales, Henry has persistent, draining conflicts with Scotland and would welcome a way of lessening or even ending these. Donald's invasion might usefully coordinate with an English attack from the south.[30] Indeed much earlier Donald alliances with English kings have been noted and if the welcomes that Donald had received at the English courts from 1378 onwards seem to have been significant, the invitation Donald received to attend Oxford may seem even more so. For back in 1378 Richard II had awarded a safe conduct lasting six years for Donald, son of John of the Isles, as a *'clericus'*, to attend that university (Latin original in Appendix I):[31]

> *Safe conduct for Donald, son of John of the Isles, clericus*
> Richard, through his accessible northern lands over a period of six years has taken into his [Richard's] safe conduct, protection and defence, Donald, the son of John of the Outer Isles in Scotland, a cleric [*clericus*] for coming into the kingdom of England through the dominion and power of Richard by land as by sea as far as the

town of Oxford at the University in that same place in studying
for his time/remaining there and thence for returning to his own
[lands]. While however the same Donald is not to try or make
to try anything which might accrue to the prejudice of Richard's
kingdom in any way whatsoever.

Donald is not described as a potential student – '*scholasticus*' – but
as a '*clericus*', the mode of address of a man of high status, clerical
or secular. Some Clan Donald historians have suggested that he did
take holy orders as a young man,[32] after his (rather un-holy) invasion
of mainland Scotland. The *Books of Clanranald* maintain that: 'He
[Donald] was an entertainer of clerics and priests and monks in his
companionship, and he gave lands in Mull and in Isla to the monastery
of Iona, and every immunity which the monastery of Iona had from
his ancestors before him; and he made a covering of gold and silver for
the relic of the hand of Columba, and he himself took the brotherhood
of the order . . .'.[33]

Donald would probably have been aged between twenty-three and
twenty-eight in 1378 when he was given the above safe conduct. This
is well over the age at which ordinary students usually began at Oxford
in mediaeval times, which was between twelve and sixteen, and the
plan seems to have been for him to study at an advanced level outside
the regular curriculum, for which six years would have sufficed. There
is indeed an entry for him under 'Isles, Donald of the', in the *Biographical Register of the University of Oxford to AD 1540*, but the only reason
for including him seems to be the existence of the 1378 safe conduct
itself.[34] The *Register*'s author Alfred Emden was exhaustive in his study
of the university, college and national records and if there was any
surviving documentary evidence of Donald actually appearing in
Oxford, he would have found it and cited it.[35]

Was the safe conduct ever in fact used? Two years previously
Donald is said to have become *de facto* Lord of the Isles, a responsi-
bility which would hardly allow of his taking six years away to study in
England. Nevertheless, the offer (bribe?) of a safe conduct for presti-
gious study in this year, which was also the year of his first appearance
at the English court, would seem to demonstrate just how much he
had been in favour with the then English king – or rather, with his
Council, for Richard (1367–1400) was but eleven years old, and only
one year on his throne.[36]

James I's Involvement?

Of any evidence that in 1411, the then English king Henry IV was involved with, or even supported Donald's mainland invasion, there is none, but had James I himself been involved? In 1407, Donald had sent an embassy 'to have colloquy with his liege lord the King of Scotland' and provided James with one of his chaplains, but there is no record of further contacts, nor of any plot of cooperation with James.[37] On the other hand we do know what James is going to do when released from English captivity in 1424, after a ransom, 'the cost' of his board and lodging of £40,000, is paid. (This is also the year after Donald's death.) Fortunately for Albany, he has died beforehand in 1420, for the returning James expresses little thanks for his bringing Donald to a standstill at Harlaw. In 1425 he tries and executes Albany's remaining family – with Donald's son on the assize.[38]

The Invasion

On having his claim to the Earldom of Ross spurned by Albany, Donald had raised an invading army of great size, for as well as calling on his islanders he could draw on the Antrim galloglasses. If the accounts of ten thousand are correct or even close, this would mean that he invaded with a highly dangerous and virtually unstoppable force, but a force with major, problematic requirements for supply and for reward, a force, furthermore, which had to achieve results before the harvest called its men home.[39] There are accounts that the army was first assembled at Ardtornish in Morvern before sailing to Strome and embarking there to march on Dingwall and seize its castle.[40]

Opposition from the likes of the Mackays of Sutherland and Caithness and Fraser of Lovat was soon overwhelmed and Inverness burned, with the people of Ross apparently acknowledging their 'real' ruler.[41] Donald now physically occupied Ross; was Albany going to hand him the title? Apparently not, and Donald is said to have felt the need or a pretext to secure his gains by extending his invasion further, as far down as the Earldom's holdings in Kincardine. Whatever the reason, his huge force now ravaged its way through Moray, Strathbogie and the Garioch, supporting itself with pillage and destruction, with the promise of the looting of wealthy Aberdeen as its reward.[42] The horrendous battle that stopped Donald in his tracks will be described in the next chapter.

The Earl of Mar

The Lord of the Isles paused on the plateau of Harlaw above Inverurie. Would Albany now face up to the reality of an unstoppable force and acknowledge his right to the Earldom? Almost certainly unknown to Donald, Albany had gambled by instructing the Earl of Mar to assemble an army and throw it against Donald in forward defence of Aberdeen, presumably in the hope that surprise would make up for any lack of numbers. In fact, the size and armament of Mar's army is not known. Romantic Lowland accounts claim odds of ten to one against his Government army, although it was a force of heavily armoured knights. One 'Highland' account even claims the 'Lowland' army was the larger – 9,700 of them against Donald's 6,600.[43]

Assembling this army below Harlaw, in the town of Inverurie, was Donald's cousin, the younger Alexander Stewart, the Earl of Mar, ostensibly an unlikely choice, for Mar's father had been the previously mentioned Alexander Stewart, notorious as the Wolf of Badenoch, leader of a force of wild caterans, who had torched Elgin Cathedral. Not surprisingly, the Wolf had never gained substantial Lowland support, and had been an open enemy of the Duke of Albany.[44] This son of his, however, had initially followed in father's footsteps as a leader of a Gaelicised military following acting in the west of Mar, but had gradually gained the confidence and support of the Lowlanders; they had even come to see him as a greater source of protection than the Duke of Albany, Governor of Scotland since 1388, had ever been able to provide.[45] Thus an initially wary Albany had begun to see Alexander as a respectable focus of authority, an agent he could trust. Expeditions and military engagements to England, France and Flanders with large retinues had helped this younger Alexander cement cooperation and service from many nobles such as Alexander, Laird of Forbes, James Scrymgeour of Dundee, and Alexander Irvine of Drum.[46]

But Mar's greatest achievement, his gaining of rank, power, lands – and respectability – was obtaining the Earldom of Mar in 1404. He has long been accused of murdering the previous Earl of Mar and of forcing the widow to marry him.[47] But whatever the truth of it, the reality lies in the approval of this new Lord of the Garioch that was shown by both Gaelic and Scots supporters.[48] Unchallenged leader of the Lowlands from the Tay to the Moray Firth, he had come to be seen as the only man capable of holding back the encroachments of

Clan Donald, and a previously wary Albany has asked him to make a stand.[49]

Albany's trust has been well rewarded, for Mar has been able to call on support from as far down as the Tay – although some of it is still to arrive. One chronicler, Bower, writes that Mar was also joined by the north-east nobles – 'all those he could have from Mar and Garioch' – yet, curiously, none of them were to be identified by the mediaeval chroniclers, other than Alexander Irvine of Drum, 'outstanding for his great strength'. [50] It even takes three hundred years before accounts of the battle start to refer even to one more North-East family – the belligerent Sir Andrew Leslie of Balquhain and his many fighting sons.[51]

Provost Davidson

One commoner member of Mar's army, heading some three dozen, ill-fated burghers from Aberdeen is also singled out by the chroniclers. This is of particular interest, for he is Robert Davidson, Provost of Aberdeen, and Mar's close friend – and fellow pirate. The North Sea is both a hive of trading activity and a rich hunting ground for pirates; Mar and Davidson seize their chances, to the anger especially of the Dutch, the Hanseatic League, and in the end, England. Davidson provided the ships, Mar provided the men (and employed any prisoners on his building projects).[52]

The Provost is a wealthy Aberdeen merchant and the owner of a tavern. Much of his wealth is lavished on the city's Kirk of Saint Nicholas, and he has served on the burgh council, and as a baillie, before twice becoming provost of the burgh, from 1405 to 1408, and from 1410 until his death at Harlaw. Only the chronicler Boece gives him the title of knighthood (which he is also awarded in an early Harlaw ballad based on Boece's account – 'And gude Sir *Robert Davidson*, Quha Provest was of *Aberdene*,' a man who 'Left to the Warld thair last gude Nicht'). That this was an honour granted on the actual battlefield, as some have suggested, is unproven.

Davidson is also collector of the customs dues of Aberdeen, channelling annuities to such as Sir Malcolm Drummond, Earl of Mar, but it will not be long before these are received by our Alexander Stewart, who marries into that Earldom in a bizarre ceremony. It takes place outside Kildrummy castle in September 1404, transforming him from a mere illegitimate son of a notorious father into a leading member of the Scottish aristocracy. Handled by Davidson, Aberdeen's customs dues now form a substantial part of the new earl's income.

The Battle

Fourteen miles from Aberdeen, on the plateau above Inverurie, on Saint James' Eve, 24 July 1411, the ferocious Battle of Harlaw between the invading force of the Lord of the Isles and the Government army led by the Earl of Mar began.

3

Early 'Highland' and Lowland Accounts of the Battle of Harlaw

This battle was fought between the forces of Donald of Islay and the Government forces of the Earl of Mar, on the plateau of Harlaw above Inverurie on Saint James' Eve, the 24th day of July, in the Julian calendar. On the modern (post-Gregorian) calendar this is the 2nd day of August. The day was a Friday, whose morning twilight at 3.15 a.m. was followed by sunrise just after 4 a.m. Its sun would set shortly after 8 p.m., with twilight extending for an hour after that. The summer night of some six hours was only little lightened by the early phase of a waxing crescent moon.

There are two sets of references, both printed and sung, to the Battle of Harlaw – those composed around the time, and those which appear many years afterwards. There are both 'Highland' and Lowland descriptions of the battle.

Early 'Highland' Accounts

When searching for printed 'Highland' references during this period, there would appear to be only three: a brief mention of the battle in contemporary Irish annals, *The Annals of Loch Cé*; an incitement to the battle – a Gaelic *brosnachadh* of some fifty lines, claimed to have been performed on the actual day; and a 1596 Campbell assessment of its outcome for the Government, *Observations of Mr. Dioness Campbell, Deane of Limerick, on the West Isles of Scotland. A.D. 1596.* Why this lack of evidence?

There would seem to be at least two good reasons. There is not only an overall scarcity of contemporary written sources, especially in Gaelic, but also, as we shall see, apart from formal charters, the administrative records of the Lords of the Isles fared especially badly. In his 1912 *Cata-*

logue of Gaelic Manuscripts in the Advocates' Library and Elsewhere in Scotland, Donald Mackinnon included in an appendix, which was headed 'Gaelic MSS. Lost or Missing', the following great regret:

1. The Records of the Isles.

During the administration of the Lords of the Isles, records seem to have been pretty regularly kept. This department, we are told, was in charge of MacDuffie or McPhee of Colonsay. These would, in part, be written in Gaelic. The disappearance of these records is a great loss not merely to the History of the West Highlands but to the History of Scotland.[1]

The Lordship of the Isles was eventually forfeited in 1493, and the powers of its last Lord removed. This resulted in a state of complete anarchy, setting in train clan conflicts, a process which appears to have resulted not only in the loss of the records of the Lordship's administration, but also the greater part of the ancient Gaelic literature.[2]

1411. The Annals of Loch Cé

The Irish annalists had no doubt as to the outcome of Harlaw, stating firmly in *The Annals of Loch Cé: A Chronicle of Irish Affairs from A.D. 1014 to A.D. 1590,* that in 1411 there was 'A great victory by Mac Dhomhaill of Alba over the Foreigners of Alba; and MacGilla-Eoin [Maclean] of Mac Dhomhaill's people was slain in the counter-wounding of that victory.'[3]

[1411?] The Brosnachadh, an Incitement to Battle

The earliest poetic work describing the Battle of Harlaw has been assumed in the past to be a Gaelic *brosnachadh,* an incitement which was supposedly sung by a MacMhuirich bard of the Macdonalds of the Isles to Donald's forces on the *actual* day of the conflict (*Là Chatha Gharbhaich*) – 'O Children of Conn remember/Hardihood in time of battle'.[4] The versions that have survived show that it was composed in the ordinary, vernacular Gaelic which would have been spoken by Donald's troops, but although Derick Thomson attempted to show that the poem was 'an authentic production of the early 15th century', it is unfortunately no longer considered to be a genuine survival from that time – more an invocation of what *should* have been delivered before the battle.

In support of that view, in their *The MacDonald Collection of Gaelic Poetry*, the Reverends MacDonald considered that although this *brosnachadh* was indeed a type of composition probably similar to others composed by the MacMhuirich bards, it 'could scarcely have been transmitted without the aid of writing'.[5] They felt that its literary finish and arrangement – each line begins with an adverbial adjective, beginning with 'a' and moving through the entire Gaelic alphabet – gave sufficient evidence that 'it could not have been composed on the spur of the moment'. It was, they considered, undoubtedly written down before Harlaw. But in this case would it have been created earlier as an 'all-purpose' incitement, or specifically composed with a possible forthcoming battle in mind?

Nothing is known of this bard, no other of his compositions have survived, yet Thomson thought it seemed 'more reasonable to conclude that Lachan Mór of Harlaw is not a ghost figure'.[6] In the University of Glasgow Library there are two manuscripts which were collected by James McLagan, chaplain to the 42nd Regiment (Black Watch) from 1764 to 1781.[7] The undated version – '*Brostughadh-Catha Chlann Domhnaill, Là Chatha Gharbhaich*' (Clan Donald's incitement to battle, on the day of the battle of Harlaw) – is ascribed to Lachlann Mór MacMhuirich, Donald's '*Aos-dàna*'. The '*Aos-dàna*', literally 'the people of the gifts', were noble learned orders dedicated to the pursuit of intellectual and artistic activities as well as crafts, on a hereditary and professional basis. Of greatest social rank and influence were the poets.[8]

As we shall see later, this manuscript also has a postscript in Scots describing the Battle of Harlaw – 'the victory was too dear to McDonald & his Highlanders'. Thomson considered this to be an addition from the first half of the eighteenth century.[9]

The other manuscript gives the author as Ian Mac Mhuirich, bard of Clanranald, and was apparently attested in 1775 by a James MacIntyre of Glenoe, 'as a true copy from an old MS. in galic [sic] character'.

Douglas Simpson, writing in 1949, postulated that Donald's army would have poured out rapidly 'like angry bees from a byke'.[10] In any case there would have been little time for a bard to assemble some ten thousand warriors and perform this magnificent but lengthy incitement. As an idealised account of what *should* have happened, it would seem to be another example of Gaelic 'reconstructions of bygone battles' – or even of totally imaginary battles.[11]

The Lament for Red Hector

There exists a pibroch listed in Gaelic as *Cumha Eachan nan Cath* (meaning in English 'Lament for Hector of the Battles') and listed in English as *Hector Roy Maclean's Lament*. Had this indeed been composed at the time, in honour of Donald's second in command, slain in mortal combat at Harlaw, it would make it the earliest known pibroch. But records of pibrochs do not appear before the seventeenth century and there can be no certainty that this one refers both to the Battle of Harlaw and the death there of Hector Maclean of Duart, or indeed perhaps to a later Maclean chief, a Hector who fell at the battle of Inverkeithing in 1651 – or that it was not composed retrospectively very many years afterwards.[12] There is even doubt as to whether the great Highland bagpipes existed at this early date.

1596. 'Observations of Mr. Dioness Campbell, Deane of Limerick, on the West Isles of Scotland. A.D. 1596'[13]

This report on the Western Isles was prepared by the Dean of Limerick for the English Secretary of State Sir Robert Cecil regarding the practicality of 'the chief of Clan Gillean', Lachlan Mor Maclean of Duart, raising loyal Scottish troops for an 'actual invasion against Tyrone, and th'other rebels in Ireland'. (As it turned out, the plan was to fall through when Lachlan Mor 'fell in a feud with his nephew, Sir James Macdonald, in 1598.)

He began with a historical account of how 'one of the sept of the McDonell' from Ulster eventually seized and occupied 'the mayne of Scotland caled Kantyre' and the countries adjoining (these now, thankfully, Campbell possessions), as well as the most part of the north of Scotland and all of the islands adjacent, 'sowth, west and northward'. Then he provided the following scathing assessment of the Macdonalds and their long-standing Ulster family connections.

> The race of the McDonells, growing to the greatness aforesaid by theire usurpation no les dishonorable than preiudicall to the state and dignetye of the Princes of Scotland, theire lords did assume as well the name of McDonell, as the title of highest dignetie, after the manner of theire Irish ancestors, their captenes doinge the like over theire families in theire several possessions as Mc Ilaine, Mc Cloyde Leos, Mc Cloyde Herres, Mc Intoshe, Mc Kennye,

Mc Hughe, O Manys, with many mo others in the Irishrye of
that land; as also presumed to geve batle unto the Kinge, whereof
one is famous by the name of the batle of Harlawe, as I have
hard, wherein the Kinges forces were overthrown and many of
his nobles . . . It may be gathered that the name dignitie and race
of the McDonells hath byn allwayes most hateful to the Princes
of Scotland, as usurpers of the patrymonie of their crowne, and
also very odious to the howse of Argeile, whose risinge grewe by
their ruyne.

Unsurprisingly, the good Dean of Limerick's recommendation was
that the 'name dignetie and forces of the MacDonalds be abolished in
favour of the ever loyal Earls of Argyll.'

Early Lowland Chronicles

Later on, in the nineteenth century, an alarmist Walter Scott was to
see Harlaw as a pivotal battle in Scotland's history:

But though the Lowlanders suffered severely, the Highlanders
had the worst and were obliged to retreat after the battle. This
was fortunate for Scotland, since otherwise the Highlanders, at
that time a wild and barbarous people, would have over-run and
perhaps actually conquered, a great part of the civilised country.[14]

The mediaeval Lowland chroniclers, however, had told a different
story. Five Lowland chroniclers – Walter Bower, John Mair, Hector
Boece, George Buchanan, and the unknown author of *Liber Pluscardensis* – provided Latin accounts written between the 1440s and
1582, of which four were quite detailed. They also have an associated
thirty-verse ballad in Scots which will be examined in Chapter 4.

c.1440s. Scotichronicon, by Walter Bower (1385–1449)[15]

Walter Bower, Abbot of Inchcolm, was persuaded to complete the
history of Scotland begun by John of Fordun, *Chronica Gentis Scotorum*
(Chronicles of the Scottish People), which had ended in 1153. He
both modified Fordun's earlier books and thereafter provided reliable
accounts of people and events in Scotland (and also in France, and to
a lesser extent in England) up until 1447. Apart from providing his

country with a good history, Bower wrote it to influence and instruct the young James II.

He gives the most contemporary account of the Battle of Harlaw. The following is from a fair copy originally belonging to Inchcolm Abbey, written in the mid 1440s and then amended under Bower's supervision until his death (the Latin version is provided in Appendix I).

Bower also produced a shortened edition (copied before 1480) of his *Scotichronicon*, known as the 'The Book of Cupar' or the 'Coupar Angus MS'.[16] Passages from it that clarify or alter the sense of the full account have been shown in italics. Additions made in the margins are shown in square brackets[17] (the Latin version is provided in Appendix I):

> In 1411 on the eve of St James the Apostle there was a battle at Harlaw in Mar, when Donald of the Isles with 10,000 men from the Isles and his men of Ross entered the district, crushing and pillaging everything and reducing it to waste. His aim on that expedition was to sack the royal town of Aberdeen and then to subject to his authority the country down to the river Tay. Since they occupied the district in such large and savage numbers like locusts, all those on domain lands who saw them were alarmed, and every man was afraid. Alexander Stewart earl of Mar went to meet him, along with Alexander Ogilvy sheriff of Angus [who always and everywhere loved justice], *with all those he could have from Mar and Garioch, Angus and the Mearns.* After a very bitter fight, the following were killed on the earl of Mar's side: the knights James Scrymgeour *constable of Dundee,* Alexander de Irvine, [Robert Melville and Thomas Murray]; William de Abernethy, son and heir of the lord of Saltoun and grandson of the governor, Alexander Straiton lord of Lauriston, George de Olgilvie heir of the lord of that Ilk, James Lovel, Alexander de Stirling and other worthy men-at-arms; and also *the warlike* Robert Davidson provost of Aberdeen with many burgesses. On the side of the Isles fell a commander called McLean, and Sir Donald the captain fled. On his side more than nine hundred were killed; on our side five hundred and nearly all the gentlemen of Buchan. [18]

The additions in italics notably increase Mar's levies 'from Angus and Mearns' ('*de Angus et Mernez*') by adding 'with all he could have from Mar and Garioch' ('*omnibus quos habere potuit de Mar et Garioch …*').[19]

A verse was also mentioned in the margin of the earlier account: 'There is a verse about this battle: In the year one thousand four hundred and ten plus one/on the eve of James was there this victory in a fight.' (*'De hoc bello metra: Anno milleno quarter c. x simul uno/ profesto Jacobi fuit hec Victoria facti.'*) It does not appear to be part of any missing ballad. It does claim, however, that there was a 'victory', which Bower's account does not.

c.1461. Liber Pluscardensis[20]

This later chronicle, by an unknown author, closely follows the first five books of Fordun's *Chronica Gentis Scotorum*, as given in Bower, with the remainder being an abridgement of the rest of the *Scotichronicon*, sometimes varying from it, but also introducing much original material, ending with the death of James I.[21] It was later referred to by George Buchanan in the tenth book of his history (see below) as *Liber Pluscardensis* ('The Book of Pluscarden'), and this name has stuck. Although written shortly after the battle, *Liber Pluscardensis* states only that:

> In the year of 1411 there was a conflict at Harlaw in the Garioch
> by Donald of the Isles against Alexander, earl of Mar, and the
> sheriff of Angus, where many nobles fell in the battle.[22]

1521. Historia Maioris Britanniae, tam Angli[a]e q[uam] Scoti[a]e, by John Mair [or Major] (c.1467–1550)[23]

A scholar highly regarded internationally for the quality of his teaching, writing and leadership, Mair wrote his history while principal of Glasgow University and canon of the Chapel Royal. It was dedicated to James V, apparently with the aim of promoting closer relationships with England. He took as his first law that for historians it was 'of more moment to understand aright, and clearly to lay down the truth on any matter, than to use elegant and highly coloured language.'[24]

Mair confirms Bower's opinion that Donald intended to sack Aberdeen and its surrounding countryside, and that the battle was extremely fiercely and highly contentiously fought, with very high numbers involved. He rejected 'the view of the common people' that Donald's 'wild Scots' (*sylvestres Scoti*) were defeated, stating that the 'annalists' (*ab annalibus* – was there another account other than Bower's around at this time?) claimed he was only forced to retreat and was not routed, despite losing more troops (nine hundred) than the Earl of Mar (six hundred), including his lieutenant Maclean, and having many of them wounded.

He claimed that the attack was organised by both the Earl of Mar and Alexander Ogilvy, Sheriff of Angus, and the following knights lost their lives: 'William Abernethy, George Ogilvy, James Scrymgeour, Alexander of Irvin, Robert Melville and Thomas Murray, together with James Lovel, Alexander Stirling and other gentlemen of lesser fame. Few combatants escaped unwounded, so intense was the fighting':

> In the year fourteen and eleven was fought that battle, far-famed amongst Scots, of Harlaw. Donald, earl of the Isles, with a valiant following of Wild Scots ten thousand strong, aimed at the spoiling of Aberdeen, a town of mark, and other places; and against him, Alexander Stewart earl of Mar and Alexander Ogilvy sheriff of Angus gathered their men, and at Harlaw met Donald of the Isles. Hot and fierce was the fight; nor was a battle with a foreign foe, and with so large a force, ever waged that was more full of jeopardy than this, so that in our games, when we were at the grammar school [Haddington; *c.* 1488], we were wont to form ourselves into opposite sides, and say that we wanted to play at the battle of Harlaw. Though it be more generally said amongst the common people that the Wild Scots were defeated, I find the very opposite of this in the chroniclers; only, the earl of the Isles was forced to retreat; and he counted amongst his men more of slain than did the civilised Scots. Yet these men did not put Donald to open rout, though they fiercely strove, and not without success, to put a check upon the audacious-ness of the man. They slew his drill-master Maklane, and other nine hundred of his men, and yet more were sorely wounded. Of the southerners six hundred only lost their lives, some of whom were gentlemen. William Abernethy, eldest-born and heir to the lord Saltoun, George Ogilvy heir to the lord of that name, James Skrymgeour, Alexander of Irvin, Robert Malvile, Thomas Muref, knights; James Luval, Alexander Stirling, with other gentlemen of lesser fame. But inasmuch as very few escaped without a wound, and the fight lasted long, it is reckoned atrocious.[25]

1527. Scotorum Historia, by Hector Boece (c.1465–1536)[26]

Boece was recruited from the University of Paris by Bishop Elphinstone to become the first Principal (and in effect, Librarian) of the University of Aberdeen, which had been newly established 'after the manner of Paris and Bologna' in 1495; he was both well liked and respected for his administrative and literary abilities. While in post he undertook a number of important publications, especially this history, published in Paris in 1527 at his own expense, and dedicated to James V. The king was so pleased with it that he awarded Boece a substantial pension and commissioned a translation into Scots.

The *Historia*, which consists of seventeen books in the form of dramatic narratives, presents the Scots as both virtuous and fiercely independent from their earliest days, and promotes devotion to duty and good government. It was to receive criticism for doubtful or unverifiable sources and was to be contrasted with Mair's history, which eschewed foundation myths and ornate writing styles.[27] It reads as follows:

> But Donald, who had as his wife an aunt of Euphemia and sister of Alexander Leslie, when he heard that Euphemia had died, claimed from the Governor the Countship/Earldom of Ross, by hereditary descent. When he [the Governor] made a reply that contained nothing that was satisfactory to him, he gathered together from the Hebrides a large body of men, partly by coercion, partly by goodwill; and taking them with him he attacked Ross-shire, and with no great trouble brought it under his own control, with the inhabitants of Ross-shire being in no way averse to taking back Donald as the rightful heir. But not content with that success, nor keeping himself within the territories which he had justly claimed, he advanced as far as Moray and Strathbogie and the areas adjacent to them, driving out the people by force, and came through the Gareotha [Garioch], being on the verge of despoiling Aberdeen, as he was threatening to do. But by encountering his aggressive behaviour in time, Alexander Stewart, illegitimate son of King Robert II, the Earl of Buchan, Earl of Mar, at Harlaw (a hamlet made famous for the most bloody battle soon waged there), engaged with him [Donald] when he [Mar] had no expectation of further reinforcements. So

it came about that when reinforcements without being in proper
order (not anticipating anything of this kind), arrived in great
disarray, very many of them were slaughtered; and so uncertain
could have been the outcome, that both sides, conceding victory,
withdrew to the nearby hills, abandoning their encampments.
Nine hundred from the Hebrideans and from those who had
attached themselves to Donald fell with Macgillan [Maclean]
and Mactothe [Macintosh], leading generals following Donald.
From the Scots on the opposing side, the nobleman Alexander
Ogilvie, viscount of Angus, a man endowed with an exceptional
sense of justice and honour, James Scrimgeour, Constable of
Dundee, a man of great spirit and outstanding virtue, famous
to later generations, Alexander Irvine of Drum, outstanding for
his great strength, Robert Maul of Panmoir, Thomas of Moray,
William Abernethy of Saltoun, Alexander Strathon of Loucen-
ston [Lauriston], Robert Davidson, provost of Aberdeen. All
these knights of high distinction, with many other nobles, lost
their lives in that battle. Donald, at once conceding victory to the
enemy, marched through the whole night, with as much speed
as he could muster, to Ross-shire, and from there by the nearest
route available, withdrew to the Hebrides.[28]

Boece raises the matter of Mar's military incompetence – attacking
without his force in full strength, and throwing in unprepared reinforcements piecemeal and not in proper battle order, troops which
were then unnecessarily slaughtered.

The Mackintosh referred to – Malcolm (Callum) Beg – in fact
survived the battle. The confusion may have been with James Mackintosh (Shaw) of Rothiemurchus, who did not.

1582. *Rerum Scoticarum Historia*, by George Buchanan (1506–82)[29]

A poet, classical scholar of international repute, administrator
and historian, who had served as tutor to the young king James VI,
Buchanan published an account of the battle in the last year of his
life.[30] He describes how the men of Ross enthusiastically fell in with
Donald, who easily invaded with ten thousand men as far as Strathbogie, threatening Aberdeen. As opposed to the views expressed in
some much later 'second set' of histories that the battle was planned

many months in advance, and had a set-piece battle formation consisting of the North-East nobility, Buchanan, like Boece, describes a highly disorganised situation involving Mar's forces of nobles from 'beyond the Tay'. This phrase *'trans Taum'* ('beyond the Tay') would not refer to the *origin* of 'all the nobility', but be part of a geographical statement about *where* Mar took his stand (*'ad Harlaum vicum'*) – though it does seem unlikely that Buchanan needed to describe the settlement of Harlaw itself as being 'beyond the Tay':

> But the second year after, which was the year 1411 AD, Donald of the Isles, Lord of the Aebudaeans [Hebrideans], sought to reclaim Ross-shire, as having been taken from him by a breach of the law on the part of the Governor, whereas he was himself the rightful heir, as indeed was true; and when he obtained no satisfaction, he gathered ten thousand of the islanders, and descended upon the mainland. He easily took possession of Ross-shire, with all the inhabitants willingly returning to the rule of their proper over-lord. But this readiness of the people of Ross-shire to comply with his rule drove his mind, which was eager for plunder, to attempt more ambitious schemes. Crossing to Moray he quickly brought it, lacking defences as it was, under his own sway. Next he crossed to Strathbogie, being intent on pillage, and now he was threatening Aberdeen. Against this sudden and unexpected adversary the Governor prepared his forces: but since the size and proximity of the threat would not allow him to wait for reinforcements coming from a great distance away, Alexander the Earl of Mar, son of Alexander brother of the Governor, with almost the entire nobility beyond the Tay, set himself to oppose him [Donald] at the hamlet of Harlaw. The battle that took place there has few equals for being both bloody and unforgettable: for the valour of noble men from all levels of society, and for the glory won in struggling against monstrous savagery. Night interrupted them, more exhausted with fighting than with the issue turning in favour of the one side or the other; and so inde-cisive was the outcome of the battle that when each side took account of which men they had lost, they reckoned that they must themselves have been the losers. For in this battle so many men, renowned for their birth and their deeds, perished; their number is exceeded by losses that are recorded in scarcely any

war, even against a foreign enemy over many years. So it came
about that a place which previously had been obscure, from that
event has become renowned to later ages.[31]

Summary of the Early Historical Accounts of
the Battle of Harlaw

When recounting what actually happened on 24 July 1411, it is all too
tempting to fill in gaps and add details which were not in fact described
at the time. An important matter, for example, which is omitted by all
the Latin chroniclers, is the number and armament of the Earl of Mar's
forces. Centuries later they are usually elaborated into a small, scratch
force of heavily-armoured and well-weaponed knights.

In 1411	Bower/Mair/Buchanan
Donald of the Isles	Bower
Earl of the Isles	Mair
Lord of the Hebrideans	Buchanan
Claimed the Earldom of Ross	Boece/Buchanan
From the Governor	Boece/Buchanan
Who refused him	Boece/Buchanan
He gathered ten thousand men	Bower/Mair/Buchanan
And won Ross-shire easily	Bower/Boece/Buchanan
Encouraging his aggression	Boece
To advance through Moray and Strathbogie to the Garioch	Boece/Buchanan
Intending to sack Aberdeen	Bower/Mair/Boece/Buchanan
And exert his authority down to the Tay	Bower
Occupying the district in large and savage numbers like locusts and everyone afraid	Bower
Of his 'Wild Scots'.	Mair
Against this sudden and unexpected adversary	Buchanan
The Governor sent	Buchanan

Alexander Stewart, Earl of Mar	Bower/Mair/Boece/Buchanan
Illegitimate son of Alexander, son of Robert II	Boece
The brother of the Governor	Buchanan
With Alexander Ogilvy, Sheriff of Angus	Bower/Mair
With almost the entire nobility beyond the Tay	Buchanan
To oppose Donald at Harlaw.	Bower/Mair/Boece/Buchanan
Mar could not wait for further reinforcements	Boece
Which had to come from a great distance away	Buchanan
Such reinforcements as came arrived in great unprepared disarray and very many slaughtered.	Boece

The fight was very bitter	Bower
Long, hot and fierce with few unwounded	Mair
With few equals as bloody and unforgettable	Buchanan
With so large a force ever waged	Mair
Full of jeopardy	Mair
With valour and nobility shown by all men	Mair
Against monstrous savagery.	Mair

Night and exhaustion ended the fight	Buchanan
So uncertain was the outcome	Boece
Both sides conceded victory	Boece
Each side reckoned they were losers	Buchanan
As so many nobles perished	Boece/Buchanan
More than ever recorded against enemy forces	Buchanan
Withdrawing to nearby hills and abandoning their encampments	Boece

Donald conceded victory, withdrew to Ross-shire and the Hebrides	Boece
But was not put to open rout	Mair
Counting more of his men slain than of Scots	Mair

Nine hundred killed of Donald's, plus many wounded	Bower/Mair/Boece
Maclean killed	Bower/Mair/Boece
And Mackintosh and leaders	Boece
Five hundred and nearly all gentlemen of Buchan killed	Bower
(six hundred, some of whom gentlemen)	Mair
Including	
Alexander Ogilvy, Sheriff of Angus	Mair
James Scrymgeour, Constable of Dundee	Bower/Mair/Boece
Alexander of Irvine	Bower/Mair/Boece
Robert Melville	Bower/Mair/Boece
Thomas Murray	Bower/Mair/Boece
William Abernethy of Saltoun	Bower/Mair/Boece
Alexander Straiton, Lord of Lauriston	Bower/Boece
George Ogilvy	Bower/Mair
Alexander Stirling	Bower/Mair
James Lovel and	Bower/Mair
Robert Davidson, Provost of Aberdeen	Bower/Boece
Donald had the victory	Loch Cé
The king's forces and many nobles were defeated.	Campbell

4

The 'Ramsay ballad': 'The Battle of Harlaw'

A lengthy ballad, 'The Battle of Harlaw', was printed in 1724 by Allan Ramsay in his *Ever Green, being a Collection of Scots Poems, wrote by the Ingenious before 1600*.[1] The term 'ballad' is used here to describe a song that tells a story. But is it acceptable to use such stories as historical evidence? As far as historical accuracy in ballads in general is concerned, opinions differ greatly. Towards the end of his life, Francis Child of Harvard, who had assembled, categorised, numbered and published his monumental *English and Scottish Popular Ballads* between 1882 and 1898, was corresponding with the Scottish ballad authority, William Walker of Aberdeen. Walker affirmed: 'I have long since come to the conclusion that the transmutations, accretions & deletions which invariably accompany traditionary lore have blurred and humbled the topography as well as the historical foundations past all identifying . . .'[2] Child himself confided in Walker: 'To tell the truth, I like to have the ballads quite in the air. It is the next best thing to their flying in the face of all history.'[3]

The late David Buchan, an authority on North-East balladry, however, suggested that ballad singers would attempt to show a truth or truths, if not necessarily *the* truth about a historical event, a suggestion that has been supported by recent examinations of ballads such as 'The Gipsy Laddie' and 'The Bonnie Earl o' Moray', which have cast fresh light on episodes of Scottish history.[4] (On the other hand, the geographically detailed Aberdeenshire 'historical' ballad 'The Bonny Lass o' Fyvie' turns out to have been a splendid confabulation of an event which took place in England, in a Derby inn.)[5]

Many, however, have accepted Francis Child's view that Ramsay's print 'was not in the least of a popular [i.e. traditional ballad] character' and had an 'artificial rhyme'.[6] The firm opinion of one North-

East traditional song authority, Gavin Greig, of this 'pseudo-ballad' was that 'the Battle of Harlaw as printed in the *Evergreen* is purely a literary production – a historical poem, and not a ballad at all in the true sense.'[7] Bertrand Bronson, who listed the tunes for fiddle and bagpipe which had titles referring to the Battle of Harlaw, even considered that 'none of the tunes ... is feasible for singing' this ballad.[8] That it was either historically accurate or even contemporary was not considered, with some even suggesting that it was written by Ramsay himself.[9] David Laing simply published the 'Ramsay' ballad, as a 'poem of considerable antiquity', despite suspicions that it was recent, claiming that 'an edition printed in the year 1668, was in the curious library of old Robert Myln'.[10] As we shall see, however, the ballad encapsulates the accounts of the conflict given by medi-aeval chroniclers, especially Boece's version. Moreover, from internal linguistic evidence it can be shown to be near contemporary with the battle itself (see Appendix II).

The Battle of *Harlaw*,

Foughten upon Friday, July 24. 1411, *against* Donald *of the* Isles.

I.

FRAE *Dunideir* as I cam throuch,
    Doun by the Hill of *Banochie*,
Allangst the Lands of *Garioch*;
    Grit Pitie was to heir and se
    The Noys and dulefum Hermonie,
That evir that dreiry Day did daw;
    Cryand the *Corynoch* on hie,
Alas ! alas ! for the *Harlaw*.

Figure 1 The opening page of the 'Battle of Harlaw' ballad, from Allan Ramsay's *Ever Green*, Edinburgh, 1724.

As can be seen from Figure 1, the actual typography is very much of Ramsay's time. Did Ramsay's printer reproduce the form of the original version? Did it have these noun capitalisations, italicisations, spelling forms and all? Or did he – or Ramsay himself – transform the original using the printing conventions of his time, for the typesetting of his preface to the *Ever Green* also uses capitalisations and italicisations? William Aytoun, in the introduction to the first volume of his *The Ballads of Scotland* (1858), stated what became the accepted view of Ramsay as 'singularly ill qualified to discharge the duty of an editor. He never felt any hesitation in altering, retouching, and adding to the old material which fell into his hands, so as to suit the prevalent taste of the age.'[11]

Aytoun, nevertheless, went on to say of Ramsay's version: 'Be that as it may the ballad deserves preservation. It is at least faithful in detail, for it recounts with minuteness the origin and incidents of the battle.' Douglas Simpson even mourned that: 'It is eloquent of the unsatisfactory state of our authorities for the battle of Harlaw that the ['Ramsay'] narrative poem should be the fullest account of the affair which we possess.'[12]

The ballad begins with a common 'As I was passing . . .' introduction, and thereafter falls into five historical sections: the cause of Donald's complaint; his initial gathering of forces to subdue Ross and invade the North-East; the account of the battle; a listing and praise of those killed on either side; and Donald's final actions and the outcome of the battle.

I.
FRAE *Dunideir* as I cam throuch,
Doun by the Hill of *Banochie*,
Allangst the Lands of *Garioch*;
Grit Pitie was to heir and se
The Noys and dulesum Hermonie
That evir that dreiry Day did daw,
Cryand the *Corynoch* on hie,
Alas! alas! for the *Harlaw*

The original Gaelic for the Garioch region, '*Gairbheach*', is pronounced roughly 'Gi-ri-och'. The last syllable eventually falls off to give 'Gi-ri-', a known feature of eastern dialects of Gaelic, at least in their declining phase. This has entered North-East Scots to give the local name and pronunciation of 'Geerie'. The balladeer, however, has used a rhyme scheme of 'Gari-och/throuch' (the 'u' being superfluous, i.e. 'throch').

William Alexander showed that a form of Gaelic – '*Garriache*'- appears in Aberdeenshire place names until 1497 at least.[13]

    The singer describes coming past the ruined fortress of Dunnideer, along the valley to the north of the hill range of Bennachie, and eventually to Inverurie. Donald himself did not come by this route; that would have meant passing the castle of Balquhain, the seat of the belligerent Sir Andrew Leslie, and his twelve (?) fighting sons who were to die in the battle.

> II.
>
> I marvlit quhat the Matter meint,
> All Folks were in a fiery fairy: ['feery-farry', state of confusion]
> I wist nocht quha was Fae or Freind;
> Zit quietly I did me carrie.   [yet]
> But sen the Days of auld King *Hairy*,
> Sic Slauchter was not hard nor sene,
> And theiar I had nae Tyme to tairy,
> For Bissiness in *Aberdene*.

It has been suggested that the friend or foe confusion was because Gaelic was the language heard on both sides of the battle, being spoken as far down as the Tay at the time.[14] Neither 'King Hairy' nor the 'Kenneth' mentioned in stanza XX have been identified with any satisfaction.[15]

> III.
>
> THUS as I walkit on the Way,
> To *Inverury* as I went;
> I met a Man and bad him stay,
> Requeisting him to make me quaint,
> Of the Beginning and the Event,
> That happenit thair at the *Harlaw*;
> Then he entreited me tak tent,   [pay attention]
> And he the Truth sould to me schaw.

Thus these three conventional introductory verses set the scene, identifying the supposed singer and his business. En route for Aberdeen, he witnesses the aftermath of a dreadful battle. Passing down through Inverurie (from where the Earl of Mar had initiated his attack), he hears the laments for the many who have been killed. None of the succinct Latin chroniclers felt the need for such an introduction.

IV.

GRIT *Donald* of the *Yles* did claim,
Unto the Lands of *Ross* sum Richt,
And to the *Governour* he came,
Them for to haif gif that he micht:
Quha saw his Interest was but slicht;
And thairfore answerit with Disdain;
He hastit hame baith Day and Nicht,
And sent nae Bodward back again.   [message]

V.

BUT *Donald* richt impatient
Of that answer Duke *Robert* gaif,
He vowd to GOD Omnipotent,
All the hale Lands of *Ross* to haif,
Or ells be graithed in his Graif.   [got ready for his grave]
He wald not quat his Richt for nocht.
Nor be abusit lyk a Slaif,
That Bargin sould be deirly bocht.

Donald's claim to the Earldom of Ross and its disdainful rejection by
Albany are documented in Boece's account of 1527 and Buchanan's
of 1582.

VI.

THEN haistylie he did command,
That all his Weir-Men should convene,   [warriors]
Ilk an well harnisit frae Hand,
To meit and heir quhat he did mein;
He waxit wrath and vowit Tein,
Sweirand he would surpryse the North,
Subdew the Brugh of *Aberdene*,
Mearns, *Angus*, and all *Fyfe*, to *Forth*.

VII.

THUS with the Weir men of the *Yles*,
Quha war ay at his bidding bown,
With Money maid, with Forss and Wyls,
Richt far and neir baith up and doun:
Throw Mount and Muir, frae Town to Town,

Allangst the land of *Ross* he roars,
And all obey'd ay his Bandown,   [command]
Evin frae the *North* to *Suthren* Shoars.

VIII.
THEN all the Countrie men did zeild;   [yield]
For nae Resistans durst they mak,
Nor offer Battill in the Feild,
Be forss of Arms to beir him bak;
Syne they resolvit all and spak,
That best it was for thair Behoif,
They sould him for thair Chiftain tak,
Believing weil he did them luve.

This depicts Donald as prepared to invade as far down as the Forth,
'subduing' (though not sacking) Aberdeen on the way. His easy occupation of Ross is confirmed, with the approval of its people, matters
which both Boece and Buchanan claimed then deluded him into
attempting such far-reaching exploits.

IX.
THEN he a Proclamation maid
All Men to meet at *Inverness*,
Throw *Murray* land to mak a Raid
Frae *Arthursyre* unto *Spey-ness.*
And further mair, he sent Express,
To schaw his Collours and Ensenzie,   [emblem]
To all and sindry, mair and less,
Throchout the Boundis of *Boyn* and *Enzie.*

X.
AND then throw fair *Strathbogie* Land,
His Purpose was for to pursew,
And quhasoevir durst gainstand,
That Race they should full fairly rew.
Then he bad all his Men be trew,
And him defend by Forss and Slicht,   [guile]
And promist them Rewardis anew,
And mak them Men of mekle Micht.

XI.
WITHOUT Resistans as he said,
Throw all these Parts he stoutly past,
Quhair sum war wae and sum war glaid,
But *Garioch* was all agast.
Throw all these Feilds he sped him fast,
For sic a Sicht was never sene;
And then, forsuith, he langd at last
To se the Bruch of *Aberdene*.   [borough]

Donald summons his lieges, fully armed. With Ross subdued and his chieftainship acknowledged, he now demands 'all men' to muster at Inverness for the invasion of Moray before sweeping down through Strathbogie and the Garioch, laying waste to these regions and terrorising the inhabitants. Unlike the ballad's author, though, all the Latin accounts emphasise that Donald's specific aim was the sacking Aberdeen – as opposed here to simply coming within sight of it.

XII.
TO hinder this prowd Enterprise,
The stout and michty Erle of MARR
With all his Men in Arms did ryse,
Even frae *Curgarf* to *Craigyvar*,
And down the syde of *Don* richt far,
Angus and *Mearns* did all convene
To fecht, or DONALD came sae nar   [before Donald came too near]
The Ryall Bruch of *Aberdene*.

Mar recruits followers both from the North-East and down to the Mearns. Two Forbes family strongholds are mentioned, the first guarding the mountain pass from the west, the second blocking a south then east approach to Aberdeen. That the chroniclers – and the ballad – make no mention of Alexander Forbes (soon to be created the premier baron of Scotland) being at the battle suggests that his crucial role was indeed to maintain his forces in position and hold the south-eastern routes to the city. This would explain Mar's eternal gratitude for the role Forbes played in the success of the battle, as carefully recorded by the Forbes family. [16]

XIII.
AND thus the Martial Erle of MARR,
Marcht with his men in richt Array,
Befoir the Enemie was aware,
His Banner bauldly did display.
For weil enewch they kend the Way,
And all their Semblance weil they saw,
Without all Dangir, or Delay,
Came haistily to the HARLAW.

This gives a very short time scale for Mar's mobilisation, but does agree with the views of both Boece ('encountering his aggressive behaviour in time'), and Buchanan ('Against this sudden and unexpected adversary').

XIV.
WITH him the braif Lord OGILVY,
Of *Angus* Sherriff principall,
The Constabill of gude *Dunde*,
The Vanguard led before them all.
Suppose in Number they war small,
Thay first richt bauldlie did pursew,
And maid thair Faes befoir then fall,
Quha then that Race did sairly rew.

XV.
AND then the worthy Lord SALTON
The strong undoubted Laird of DRUM,
The stalwart Laird of *Lawristone;*
With ilk thair forces all and sum.
PANMUIR with all his men did cum,
The Provost of braif *Aberdene*,
With Trumpets and with Tuick of Drum,
Came schortly in thair Armour schene.   [bright]

XVI.
THESE with the Erle of MARR came on,
In the Reir-ward richt orderlie,
Thair Enemies to sett upon;
In awfull Manner, hardily,

Togither vowit to live and die,
Since they had marchit mony Mylis
For to suppress the Tyrannie
Of douted Donald of the *Yles*.

All the chroniclers other than Buchanan agree that the Earl of Mar, together with Alexander Ogilvy, assembled and led a force to oppose Donald, but the limited list of only seven other Lowland leaders in the ballad comes from Boece's account. The balladeer, however, makes no mention of the detailed account of Mar's tactical incompetence as described by Boece and Buchanan.

XVII.
BUT he in Number Ten to Ane,
Richt subtilie alang did ryde,
With *Malcomtosch* and fell *Maclean*,
With all their Power at thair Syde,
Presumeand on thair Strenth and Pryde,
Without all Feir or ony Aw,
Richt bauldlie Battil did abyde,
Hard by the Town of fair HARLAW.

XVIII.
THE Armies met, the Trumpet sounds,
The dandring Drums alloud did touk,
Baith Armies byding on the Bounds,
Till ane of them the Feild sould bruik.   [possess]
Nae Help was thairfor, nane wald jouk,   [avoid]
Ferss was the Fecht on ilka Syde.
And on the Ground lay mony a Bouk   [corpse]
Of them that thair did Battill byd.

XIX.
WITH doutsum Victorie they dealt,
The bludy Battil lastit lang,
Each Man his Nibours Forss thair felt;
The weakest aft-tymes gat the Wrang;
Thair was nae Mowis their them amang,   [light-heartedness]
Naithing was hard but heavy Knocks,
That Eccho maid a dulefull Sang,
Thairto resounding frae the Rocks.

This is the first mention of Mar's force being only a tenth of the size of Donald's. All the chroniclers agree that the battle was an extremely bitter fight with great slaughter on both sides, and that Maclean ('Red Hector of the Battles') was Donald's lieutenant. Macintosh, however, only appears in Boece's account.

XX.
BUT *Donald's* men at last gaif back;
For they war all out of Array.
The Earl of MARRIS Men throw them brak,
Pursewing shairply in thair Way,
Thair Enemys to tak or slay,
Be Dynt of Forss to gar them yield,
Quha war richt blyth to win away,
And sae for Feirdness tint the Feild.

XXI.
THEN *Donald* fled, and that full fast,
To Mountians hich for all his Micht;
For he and his war all agast,
And ran till they war out of Sicht;
And sae of *Ross* he lost his Richt,
Thocht mony Men with him he brocht,
Towards the *Yles* fled Day and Nicht
And all he wan was deirlie bocht.

XXII.
THIS is, (quod he) the richt Report
Of all that I did heir and knaw,
Thocht my Discourse be sumthing short,
Tak this to be a richt suthe Saw: [truthful account]
Contrairie GOD and the Kings Law,
Thair was spilt mekle Christian Blude,
Into the Battil of *Harlaw*;
This is the Sum, sae I conclude.

Although the balladeer appears to have been following Boece's account so far – that the outcome of the battle was dubious – he does not include Boece's description of *both* sides withdrawing to the nearby hills, and that only thereafter did Donald retire swiftly to his home territory.

XXIII.
BUT zit a bony Quhyle abyde
And I sall mak thee cleirly ken
Quhat Slauchter was on ilkay Syde,
Of *Lowland* and of *Highland* Men,
Quha for thair awin haif evir bene: [own sides]
These Lazie Lowns micht weil be spaird,
Chessit lyke Deirs into thair Dens,   [misspelt 'e'? i.e., 'dene' = dingle]
And gat thair Waiges for Rewaird.

XXIV.
MALCOMTOSH of the Clan Heid Chief,
Macklean with his grit hauchty Heid,
With all their Succour and Releif,
War dulefully dung to the Deid:
And now we are freid of thair Feid,   [feud]
They will not lang to cum again;
Thousands with them without Remeid,
On *Donald*'s Syd that Day war slain.

Maclean's body was carried from the field to be buried in Iona, but as noted earlier the Mackintosh here referred to – Malcolm (Callum) Beg – in fact survived the battle. The confusion may have been with James Mackintosh (Shaw) of Rothiemurchus, who did not.

XXV.
AND on the uther Syde war lost,
Into the Feild that dismal Day,
Chief Men of Worth (of mekle Cost)
To be Lamentit sair for ay.
The Lord *Saltoun* of *Rothemay*,
A Man of Micht and mekle Main;
Grit Dolour was for his Decay,
That sae unhappylie was slain.

Bower and Mair both correctly state that it was not Lord Saltoun who was killed, but his heir. The ballad has apparently followed Boece's claim that Lord Saltoun himself was killed.

XXVI.

OF the best Men amang them was,
The gracious gude Lord OGILVY,
The Sheriff-Principal of *Angus*;
Renownit for Truth and Equitie,
 For Faith and Magnanimitie;
He had few Fallows in the Field,
Zit fell by fatall Destinie,
For he nae ways wad grant to zeild.

Bower and Mair correctly state that it was Alexander Ogilvy, Lord
Ogilvy's heir, who was killed, not Lord Ogilvy, Sheriff of Angus. Again,
the ballad's error first appears in Boece.

XXVII.

SIR *James Scrimgeor* of *Duddap*, Knicht,
 Grit Constabill of fair *Dunde*,
Unto the dulefull Deith was dicht,   [struck]
The Kingis cheif Banner-man was he,
A valziant Man of Chevalrie,
Quhais Predecessors wan that Place
At *Spey*, with gude King WILLIAM frie,
Gainst *Murray* and *Macduncans* Race.

XXVIII.

GUDE Sir *Allexander Irving*,
The much renownit laird of *Drum*,
 Nane in his Days was better sene,
Quhen they war semblit all and sum;
To praise him we sould not be dumm,
 For Valour, Witt and Worthyness,
To end his days he ther did cum,
Quhois Ranson is remeidyless.

XXIX.

AND thair the Knicht of *Lawriston*
Was slain into his Armour schene,
And gude Sir *Robert Davidson*,
Quha Provest was of *Aberdene*,
The Knicht of *Panmure*, as was sene,

A mortall Man in Armour bricht,
Sir *Thomas Murray* stout and kene,
Left to the Warld thair last gude Nicht.

Neither Bower nor Mair claim that Provost Davidson was a knight. Once more, this mistake in the ballad is first made in Boece's chronicle. The eight slain knights are as listed by Boece.

XXX.
THAIR was not sen King *Keneths* Days
Sic strange intestine crewel Stryf
In *Scotland* sene, as ilk Man says,
Quhair mony liklie lost thair Lyfe;   [fine men]
Quhilk maid Divorce twene man and Wyfe,
And mony Childrene fatherless,
Quhilk in this Realme has bene full ryfe;
LORD help these Lands, our Wrangs redress.

XXXI.
IN *July*, on Saint *James* his Even,
That four and twenty dismall Day,
Twelve hundred, ten Score and eleven
Of Zeirs sen CHRYST, the Suthe to say: [years]
Men will remember as they may,
Quhen thus the Veritie they knaw,
And mony a ane may murn for ay,
The brim Battil of the *Harlaw*.   [fierce]

Seemingly unaware of many of the contents of Bower's and Mair's accounts, the balladeer makes mistakes, i.e. concerning Lauriston, Ogilvy, the knighting of Davidson and the battlefield rout and flight of Donald. All of these errors first appear in Boece's history.

Such evidence convinced both Norval Clyne and Gavin Greig that the ballad was based on a reading of Boece.[17] If this was the case, however, why are highly important details which Boece gave – such as Mar's failures in command and the withdrawal of both sides from an undecided battlefield – missing from this ballad? It would appear that the balladeer was not working from Boece's original Latin history, but an abbreviated version made by John Bellenden:

Bellenden prepared two major vernacular versions of Hector
Boece's *Scotorum historia* (1527): the first, commissioned by
the king, survives in manuscript, and was finished in 1531; the
other was printed by Thomas Davidson in Edinburgh *c*.1536, and
it may also be the 'new cronikle' presented to James V in 1533
... Neither version is an entirely reliable witness to Boece's text,
and while the two versions are obviously connected, not least by
intermediate manuscripts, they are far from identical ... Many
of Bellenden's alterations may be of his own devising, since they
do not appear in the 1574 edition of the *Scotorum historia*, nor
do they correspond with Boece's style. Nevertheless, Bellenden's
translation was highly influential on the way in which the Scots
regarded themselves.[18]

Bellenden's translation of Boece's account of Harlaw repeats all of
Boece's errors, but omits important details such as his criticism of the
Earl of Mar's battle tactics:

Donald of the Ilis, herand his wiffis ant deceissit, come to Duke
Robert desiring the landis of Ros to be gevin to him, as nerrest
and lauchfull heritour thairto. Nochtheles, he gat not bot repuls
[evill ansuere fra the Governour]: and, thairfore, he come,
with all the power of the Ilis, and subdewit Ros to his opinion
[empire]. Nocht content of thir boundis, he come throw Murray,
Bogheval, and sindry othir boundis lyand thairabout; syne come
to Garioch, to birne Abirdene.
[In the menetyme] To punis thir attemptatis, come Alexander Stewart, Erle of Marre [bastard son to Alexander Erle of
Buchquhan, quhilk was son to King Robert the Second], and
faucht aganis the said Donald at Harlaw [with uncertan victory],
quhair [and sa huge] gret slauchter was maid on all sides [that thai
war constrenit to seveir and fle to the montanis]. In this battall,
DCCCC Hielandmen war slane; with Makclane and Mackinthos,
principal capitanis under Donald of the Ilis. And of the Erle of
Marris side, war slane Alexander Ogilvy, seref of Angus; James
Skrimgeour, Constabil of Dunde; Alexander Irrewin of Drum;
Robert Mald of Panmure; Thomas Murray; William Abirnethy of
Saltoun; Alexander Straitoun of Lourestoun; Robert Davidstoun,
Provest of Abirdene, – knichtis; with mony othir. This battall was

strikin on Sanct James Evin, the yeir of God, MCCCCXI yeris. Donald, efter his discomfitoure, [past with grete deligence the samyn nycht to Ross, and eftir that] fled with gret deligence to the Ilis. Nochtheles, Duke Robert persewit the said Donald so scharply, that he come in [to his] wil, efter that he was sworn nevir to invade the realme [agane with ony iniuris] with mair trubill.[19]

It was this translation of Boece into Scots that the ballad maker used for the core of his song, expanding the account with flourish and verve using phrases and tropes from a well-stocked ballad kitty to enhance his own memorable lines, such as 'Left to the Warld thair last gude Nicht'. Was all this padding from his imagination, or was he calling on still remembered traditional accounts? Indeed, had he access to now lost writings?

The Purpose of the 'Ramsay ballad'?

Apparently dating from between the 1530s and 1548 (when Douglas Simpson said it was 'known to have been in existence'),[20] the 'Ramsay ballad' could therefore have been composed during the reigns of James V (1513–1542) or Mary Queen of Scots (1542–1567). The most likely is that of James V:

> James V was a keen musician. He played the lute, could sight-read vocal scores, and employed a large staff of musicians and minstrels . . . The literary patronage of the court was of a remarkably high quality. During the minority both John Mair and Hector Boece dedicated their histories of Scotland (1521 and 1527 respectively) to the king. Both works were scholarly neo-Latin tomes with humanist influences, but Mair's work, which advocated a union of the realms of England and Scotland, did not find favour with the adult king, who preferred the forthright nationalism of Boece. James commissioned John Bellenden to translate Boece's history and Livy's *History of Rome* into Scots. Many poets were patronized by the king . . .[21]

Interestingly, James V also commissioned a verse translation of Boece's chronicle, from the courtier and poet William Stewart, which remained in manuscript form until 1858. Its somewhat skimpy rendering of the Battle of Harlaw section, however, is not the 'Ramsay ballad'.[22] Politically, James' priority seems to have been to enforce royal authority and justice throughout the realm. His lieutenant of the north, the Earl of Moray, was bringing order to Caithness and Sutherland, but his lieutenant of the west, the 4th Earl of Argyll, was failing to control Maclean of Duart and Macdonald of Islay. In 1531 the king planned a show of strength in the west; an army was to gather under James' command to meet up with a force under Moray for a joint campaign, but this seems to have been cancelled when Macdonald and Maclean submitted to the king.

In these contexts, the composition and singing of a ballad based on the writings of the king's favourite historians, triumphantly recounting how the ancestors of Macdonald and Maclean were brought to heel in the past, would have been highly opportune.

It is not possible to say that the popular song, apparently about Harlaw, which was in circulation during the mid sixteenth century and mentioned in *The Complaynt of Scotland*, was the above 'Ramsay ballad'. It depicts a group of shepherds and their wives amusing themselves by singing 'sueit melodious sangis of natural music of the antiquite', one of which was entitled 'the battel of the hayrlau'. Only the title of the song was given, however, and no verses.[23]

Part 2

The Much Later Accounts

5

The Seventeenth and Early Eighteenth-century Accounts

Post-1660s. *The* [Sleat] *History of the Macdonalds, by Uisdean (Hugh) MacDonald*[1]

Although this history extends roughly from 1100 to 1500, it must have been written after 1628, for it refers to an earl whose patent dates from that year. As its purpose is to demonstrate that the Macdonalds had always been loyal to the Scottish Crown, a date after the Restoration of Charles II in 1660 (or even his early Scottish crowning at Scone in 1651) would seem better. Written in English, it was bitterly opposed to the accounts given by Boece and Buchanan: 'These partial pickers of Scotish chronology and history [who] never spoke a favourable word of the Highlanders, much less of the Islanders and Macdonalds.'

Written by one who 'clearly had access to the charter chests of the Macdonalds of Sleat', the most likely author was an amateur historian, a Captain Uisdean MacDonald from North Uist, who belonged to the ruling lineage of the Macdonalds of Sleat and North Uist (and is scathing about other branches of the Macdonalds, especially those of Glengarry who had had the temerity to dispute the right of the Sleat line to the headship of the clan).[2] With 'its broad range of sources, haphazard organisation, racy polemicism and unabashed partisanship' this history appears to have been written for a Scottish and British legal audience at a time when there was a need to provide quasi-legal status and function as Scots law exerted a more powerful grip over the Highlands, 'squeezing out the distinctive, indigenous legal and customary practices' and appeals to rights to territories based on continuous possession from time immemorial in direct and unbroken male descent (with no taint of tanistry).

Its preamble outlines the descent of the Macdonalds from Somerled, complaining that Buchanan – 'a Highlander' (i.e. a Gaelic speaker) never spoke anything good . . . of the Highlanders, much less of the Islanders' and that Boece constantly related that the king went on to suppress rebellion here and there, especially in the Isles, 'whereas it is well known that the Islanders are as loyal and less injurious to their neighbours than any people in Scotland'.

He [Donald] married Margaret Lesly, daughter of William Lesly, Earl of Ross, who had no children except her and a son called Alexander. This Alexander was married to the Duke of Albany's daughter, left no issue but one daughter named Eupheme. She being very young, the governor, her grandfather, took her to his own family, and having brought her up, they persuaded her by flattery and threats to resign her rights of the Earldom of Ross to John, his second son, Earl of Buchan, as it was given out, and *that* much against her will. But others were of the opinion that she did not resign her rights; but thereafter she was bereaved of her life, as most men thought by the contrivance of the governor. Donald, Lord of the Isles, claimed right to the Earldom of Ross, but could get no other hearing from the governor, but lofty menacing answers; neither could he get a sight of the rights which the Lady Eupheme gave to his son, John. The governor thought that his own sway and strength could carry everything according to his pleasure in the kingdom, still hoping for the crown, the true heir thereof (James I, nephew to the Duke of Albany) being prisoner in England. He likewise was at emnity with the Lord of the Isles, because Sir Adam Moor's daughter was his grandmother, knowing right well that he would own his own true heir's cause against him. The Lord of the Isles told the governor he would either lose all he had or gain the Earldom of Ross, to which he had such a good title. The Duke replied he wished Donald would be so forward as stick to what he said.

This appears to be the first detailed description of both Donald's claim to the Earldom of Ross and of Albany's forcing the Ross heiress to give it to his son John. Not only that, but the all-powerful governor is described as not only guilty of her murder thereafter, but also of having hopes of becoming king. Euphemia was still alive at the time of the battle, and only resigned the Earldom three years after it in 1414. Boece merely said that Albany's response to Donald's claim was not 'satisfactory'; this account claims it was aggressively provocative. The scene began to be set:

> Donald immediately raised the best of his men, to the number of 10,000, and chose out of them 6600, turning the rest to their homes. They thought first they would fight near Inverness, but, because the duke and his army came not, Donald's army marched through Murray and over the Spey. The governor, Alexander Stewart, Earl of Murray, and John Stewart, Earl of Buchan, the governor's son, having gathered an army of 9700 men, desired the Lord of the Isles to stay, and that they would meet them near Inverness and give him battle.

This is a dramatic change. Donald is depicted as having the smaller force, albeit of picked men, with the government army being very much greater. The Alexander Stewart who raised his force was not Governor Albany himself, but his illegitimate son, the Earl of Mar. The Earl of Buchan was not present. This is the first account which gives a size for Mar's army – 9,700 men. This is a indeed a very great number, not mentioned by the Latin chroniclers; it might seem unlikely, but there was no other description of its size made at the time.

> But he [Donald] would not leave his own men foraging in his own country of Ross. Therefore he marched forward, resolving to take his hazard near their [Mar's] doors, assuring himself of victory. Huntly, who was Macdonald's friend, sent him a private message, desiring him to commit no hostilities in his [Huntly's] country, by way of assuring him he would not own the governor's quarrels, and wishing Donald good success and desiring him to be of good courage.

Thus Donald's march down to meet the opposition is purely to spare his newly acquired county of Ross from foragers (although as the Ross exclaves extend through the North-East down to Kincardine they will instead get the brunt of this as he marches through them). This is the only time a supportive Huntly is brought on to the scene; there is no other evidence that this Gordon earl was involved in such a friendly way, keeping Donald's left flank free from the threat of attack.

The Lord of the Isles went forward till both armies met at Harlaw, a place in Garrioch, in the Braes of Buchan. There came several in the governor's army out of curiosity to see Macdonald and his Highlanders routed; others came to be rewarded by the governor as they did not expect to see any other king in all appearance, but he and his offspring; others came through fear of the Duke's authority.

There is no record of the Duke of Albany being present, nor is there any evidence that Mar's supporters came along either for entertainment or in the hope of making the Duke king, or even because they feared to disobey him.

Macdonald set his men in order of battle as follows. He commanded himself the main battle, where he kept most of the Islanders, and with the Macleods, John of Harris and Roderick of Lewis. He ordered the rest to the wings, the right commanded by Hector Roy Maclean, and the left by Callum Beg Macintosh, who that day received from Macdonald a right of the lands of Glengary in Lochaber, by way of pleasing him for yielding the right wing to Maclean, and to prevent any quarrel between him and Maclean. MacIntosh said he would take the lands and make the left behave as well as the right. John More, Donald's brother, was placed with a detachment of the lightest and nimblest men as a reserve, either to assist the wings or the main battle, as occasion required. To him was joined Mackenzie and Donald Cameron of Locheill. Alister Carrich was young, and therefore was much against his will set apart, lest the whole of the brothers should be hazarded at once.

Only a hundred and fifty years after the battle it may well be that disposition of Donald's captains – and their great sensitivity to battle rights – is accurate, perhaps because they had been held firmly in oral memory.

It is interesting to compare these dispositions with a later account of Culloden, where the Macdonalds were 'unfortunately placed on the left and not the right wing'. Angus Macdonald, Lord of the Isles, had been placed on the right by Bruce at Bannockburn and had enjoyed that honour ever since, 'except when it was given up to the Laird of MacLean at the battle of Harlaw'.[3]

The Earls of Marr and Buchan ordered their men in a main battle and two small fronts: the right wing was commanded by the Lord Marischal and Erroll; the left by Sir Alexander Ogilvie, Sheriff of Angus. They encountered on another; their left wing was forced by MacLean and the party on Macdonald's right [i.e. the Lowland right wing] was forced to give way. There was a great fold for keeping cattle behind them, into which they went. The Earl of Marr was forced to give ground, and that wing was quite defeated. Marr and Erroll posted to Aberdeen, the rest of Macdonald's men followed the chase. There were killed on the governor's side 2550. The Lord Marishall was apprehended safe, and died in his confinement of mere grief and despair.

These are the first and only mentions of Keith, the Earl Marischal, and Errol, the Constable of Scotland, although the Keith family annals are said to claim that it was Alexander, the third son of the aged Earl Marischal who fought at Harlaw.[4] The flight, however, of them both to Aberdeen, with Keith then dying of grief, is a fable.

Sir Alexander Ogilvy, Sheriff of Angus, was killed with seven knights, and several other gentlemen. On Macdonald's side Maclean fell; he and Irvin of Drum fought together until one killed the other. Drum's two brothers, with the principal men of that surname, were killed, so that a boy of the name that herded the cattle, succeeded to the estate of Drum. Two or three gentlemen of the name of Munroe were slain, together with the son of Macquarry of Ulva, and two gentlemen of the name of Cameron.

This appears to be the first account of the story of the death in mutual combat of Hector Maclean of Duart and Alexander Irvine of Drum (the only North-East noble mentioned in the Latin accounts). As will be seen later, it is also recorded in the likes of the Irvine-Fortescue papers of the 1720s, and in 1734 Clan Maclean histories (below). The fate of the brothers and of the estate is imaginary.

On Macdonald's side were lost in all 180. This battle was fought 1411. Macdonald had burnt Aberdeen, had Huntly not dissuaded him from it, saying that by his victory in all appearance he gained his won, yet it was ridiculous to him to destroy the town, and that citizens would always join with him who had the upper hand. Now to prove [test] these fabulous and partial writers, particularly Buchanan, it is well known to several men of judgement and knowledge, that Macdonald had the victory there, and gained the Earldom of Ross for four or five generations thereafter, and that MacIntosh, whom they say was killed, lived twenty years thereafter . . .

Neither Donald nor any of his men ever got beyond Harlaw to threaten Aberdeen, and Huntly's supposed intercession would not have been necessary. Admittedly its citizens had a reputation for supporting a winner; they benefited greatly when they supported Bruce in his brutal devastation of Aberdeen's hinterland in his struggle against the Comyns. Buchanan had not in fact reported that MacIntosh had been killed.

Thus according to the this seventeenth-century historian, at the Battle of Harlaw Mar's superior force was broken and fled to Aberdeen, with only concealed cowards thereafter creeping out on the battlefield for petty plundering. But as we shall see, this historian's worst confabulation, the very opposite of Harlaw's dismal aftermath was: 'After the battle Macdonald returned again to the Isles, no opposition being made to him all his lifetime in Ross.'

The Red and Black Books of Clanranald[5]

These manuscripts appear to be the only prose description of the Battle of Harlaw in Scottish Gaelic, although they did not get written down until the early eighteenth century. After the Lordship of the Isles was forfeited in 1493 and its territory dismembered, there was a deliberate and thorough destruction of its the physical and cultural heritage. Although the *Red Book* and the *Black Book* were written after the Lordship was long gone, they were part of a literary tradition begun centuries earlier, and contained material which was certainly composed and written down well within the period of the Lordship. The *Red* and *Black Books* – neither are actual books – consist of manuscripts written on paper by the professional poets and historians to the old Highland nobility who composed them in a literary dialect known as 'Classical Gaelic'. Most importantly, they contain a 'History of Clan Donald' which includes Donald's action at Harlaw.

The *Red Book of Clanranald* was compiled by Niall MacMhuirich of South Uist, a member of the family that had provided poets and chroniclers to the Clan Donald and Clanranald chiefs. The *Black Book* (which is not 'of Clanranald') has a number of authors, in particular Christopher Beaton, *Gille Críost Mac Bheathadh*, a member of a Gaelic learned family who provided medical services to the Macleans and several other Gaelic ruling families, but which also included a number of members who joined other professions, including the Church and literature. Beaton made the *Black Book* as a copy of the *Red Book* for his own use.

Both sets of manuscripts, MCR39 and MCR40, are currently held by the National Museum of Scotland; there are no copies of either in the National Library. There is also considerable doubt as to whether the '*Red*' book is in fact the original *Red Book* – the *Leabhar Dearg* of Clanranald which was said to have been lent to James Macpherson for the Ossianic poems it held. The *Red Book* manuscripts held by the National Museum have thus been described alternatively as the '*Little Book*'.[6] Although it was said to have been returned to Clanranald, it was also claimed to have been taken thereafter by emigrants to Australia, where in the 1930s a woman said she owned this book – but unfortunately could not be persuaded to show it to scholars.[7]

The Reverend Donald Macintosh made a transcript and English translation of the historical portions of the *Red Book* which was used by various writers such as Walter Scott, but the best known transcriptions and translations of the *Black* and *Red Books* appear in the second volume of the 1894 *Reliquiae Celticae*, a collection of 'texts, papers and studies in Gaelic literature and philology' initiated by the Reverend Alexander Cameron and edited after his death by Alexander MacBain and John Kennedy. The only reference in this edition to Donald of Isla at Harlaw in the *Black Book* contains the phrase: '*Do bhrisd se cath gaifech ar Dhiúc Murchadh*', literally, 'He broke the battle of Garioch against Duke Murdoch', but which is translated only as, 'He fought the battle of Garrioch or Harlaw against Duke Murdoch'.[8]

A fresh translation of the entire entry concerning Donald, however, reads as follows:

We now come to Donald of Isla, son of John, son of Angus Og, the brother of Ranald, how he took the Lordship with the consent of his brothers and the nobles of the Isles. All other persons were obedient to him, and he married Mary, daughter of the Earl of Ross, and it is from her side that the Earldom of Ross came to the Macdonalds. He was styled Earl of Ross and Macdonald, and Lord of the Isles. There are many exploits and deeds written of him in other places. He won the battle of Garrioch over duke Murdoch, defending his own rights against him in the matter of the Earldom of Ross, and on the return of King James the First from the captivity of the King of England, Donald of Isla obtained the king's agreement and confirmation to Ross and the rest of his titles, and duke Murchadh and his son were beheaded.

He [Donald] was one who kept clerics and priests and monks in his companionship, and he gave lands in Mull and in Isla to the monastery of Iona, and every immunity which the monastery of Iona had from his ancestors before him; and he made a covering of gold and silver for the relics of the hand of Columba, and he himself took the brotherhood of the order, having left a lawful and suitable heir in the sovereignty of the Isles and of Ross, viz., Alexander, son of Donald. He afterwards died in Isla, and his fully noble body was interred on the south side of the church of Oran [Iona].[9]

Leaving aside the fact that Donald's opponent was actually the duke of Albany, and not his son Murdoch (a confusion also made in the 1838 Clan Maclean history in Chapter 7), the significant difference in the above fresh translation is that Donald actually *won* the Battle of Harlaw.

But there is more to it than that. The Gaelic in the *Red Book* reads: '*Do brisd se cath Gaifech cairfech ar diúc Murchadh . . .*'[10] Again, this would literally be, 'He broke the battle of Garioch against Duke Murdoch', but the scribe has also qualified the battle as '*cairfech*'. This will be the Irish Gaelic adjective '*gáibhtheach*', with its meanings of 'dangerous, terrible, fierce, eager, exaggerating, costly, distressed, pitiful, plaintive'.[11] (It survives in Modern Irish as '*gáifeach*'.) In other words, this comes close to describing the battle as a Pyrrhic victory, and offers a number of possible outcomes for Donald:

'He won the costly Battle of Harlaw against Duke Murdoch.'
'He won a narrow/Pyrrhic victory over Duke Murdoch at the
    Battle of Harlaw.'
'He won the fiercely fought/terrible Battle of Harlaw against
    Duke Murdoch.'

These versions are a long way from claiming that Donald merely 'fought' the Battle of Harlaw, and confirm the opinions of the 'Sleat historian' and of Macdonald historians in general, that he did indeed have a victory there, although at a terrible cost. There is no suggestion that the adjective *'cairfech'* – 'dangerous, terrible, fierce' – referred to any 'wild Highlanders'.

The Addendum in English to the *Brosnachadh*[12]

The manuscript of the version of the *Brosnachadh* ascribed to Ian Mac Mhuirich, bard of Clanranald, and attested in 1775 by a James MacIntyre of Glenoe 'as a true copy from an old MS. in galic character', has this postscript in Scots written on its back, possibly by the antiquarian Walter MacFarlane in the first half of the eighteenth century.[13]

> There was more noble blood shed in this battle (incomparably) than in any fought in Scotland for three centuries – There were 30 Noblemen slain therein & about 16 Tribes of the Low country people quite extirpat. The retreat was followed 14 miles from the first stance of battle whereon they began, yet at ilka mile's rout they rallied, so that victory was too dear to McDonald & his Highlanders. It was both fateague & darkness of the night that parted them. McDonald settled all Ross after the battle; and after the king came home from his imprisonment, he executed all those of his subjects that occasioned this cruel and unjust trouble in his absence & was instrumental in destroying such a number of his valiant subjects in an unjust cause.

For the first time the picture is painted of Mar's army being forced to retreat fourteen miles, but resisting and rallying so well that Donald judged that defeating them would be too costly. Fourteen miles is a considerable exaggeration; it would have taken Mar and his men well off the plateau of Harlaw and as far as the outskirts of Aberdeen. Again, night and weariness terminated the battle and neither side claimed victory in a confrontation with a dreadful loss of Lowland life. In a startling way, James I is portrayed as returning with a vengeance to destroy those who had caused such damage to his subjects 'in an unjust cause', i.e. Albany and his followers in resisting Donald and his rightful claim to the Earldom.

1715. *The Martial Atchievements* [sic] *of the Scots Nation,* by Patrick Abercromby MD

Born in Forfar, Abercromby (1656–c.1716 onwards) seems to have been educated both privately and at Catholic institutions on the Continent, including Douai and perhaps Paris, before returning to Scotland to take the degree of MD at St Andrews University in 1685. Appointed physician to James VII and II, he lost this post at the revolution in 1688, spending time abroad before returning during the reign of Queen Anne to settle in Edinburgh, a confirmed Jacobite, and devote himself to the study of Scottish history and antiquities. His most important work was *The Martial Atchievements of the Scots Nation* from 1329 to 1514, published in two volumes in 1711 and 1715. Most of the early history in the first volume is now regarded as purely mythical, but the remainder contained evidence of genuine biographical and historical research, although biased towards a markedly royalist view of history.[14] Volume II contains the following description of Donald's invasion – this time, however, in league with England:

> Donald of the Isles, being abundantly satisfied of the justice of his cause, and strengthened by his alliance with King Henry, whose forces made no small diversion in the south parts of Scotland, thought it no high time to break in upon the North. With this view he raised an army of no less than 10000 men within his own isles, and setting himself at their head made a descent on the continent, and without opposition seized on the land in debate, they of Ross being willing to return to the subjection of their rightful master. This success did not satisfy the mind of Donald, who judging that he could not long keep what was his own, without a barrier sufficient to skreen him from the superior Power by which he conceived himself so heinously injured; and perhaps being by his league with England obliged to do all the mischief he could to the kingdom of Scotland, he continued his march from Ross to Murray, and from thence to Strathbogy and Garioch, ravaging these countries as he passed through them, and threatening to enrich his men with the wealth of Aberdeen, a trading town and a bishop's seat.
>
> But before he could reach that place, he found himself stopt in his career by Alexander Stewart, a grandchild of king Robert

II by consequence the Governour's nephew, and earl of Marr . . . That brave and experienced general, by orders of the Governour, drew together with great Expedition, almost all the Nobility and Gentry between the two Rivers of Tay and Spey, consisting chiefly, as they still do, of the *Lyons, Ogilvies, Maules, Carnegies, Lindsays, Erskines, Fotheringhams, Leslies, Frazers, Irvines, Gordons, Forbesses, Abercrombies, Bannermans, Arbuthnots, Burnets, Leiths, Duguds, Mowats, Barclays, etc.* Being seconded by these, he met the invader at Harlaw, a village in the Garioch, within 10 miles of Aberdeen, where a long, uncertain and bloody Battle ensued; so long that nothing but Night could put an end to it; so uncertain, that it was hard to tell who had lost or win the Day; and so bloody that, to say nothing of the loss sustained by the Highlanders, almost the whole gentry of *Angus, Merns, Marr, Buchan* and *Garioch* were cut off;[15] insomuch that one family of the sirname of *Lesly*, I mean that of Balwhain, is by tradition reported to have lost . . . Lesly the father and 6 of his 7 sons.

Vast numbers of others had the same fate, among the rest Alexander Ogilvy Sheriff of Angus, together with his son and heir, James Scrimgeour Constable of Dundee, Alexander Irvine of Drum, Thomas Maule of Panmuir, William Abernethey you[n]ger of Salton, Alexander Straiton of Lawrieston, Alexander Stirling, Thomas Murray, and Robert Davidson, provost of Aberdeen, all knights, and some of them chiefs of honourable and loyal families still extant in those parts. They of the earl of Marr'*s* party who survived, lay all night on the Field of Battle; while Donald, being rather wearied with action, than conquered by force of arms, thought fit to retreat, first to *Ross*, and then to the Isles; which he effected without any considerable molestation, by reason that the shattered forces in the North were not in a condition to pursue him, and those expected from the south and west were not yet come up. The petty war which was carried on at the same time against England no doubt retarded the motion of these last, and hindred the Governour from acting with that vigour that was necessary, either against the domestic rebels (for so he and the bulk of the nation called the Lord of the Isles and his adherents,) or the foreign enemies of the kingdom: . . .

The author has extended greatly the basic histories given by the Latin chroniclers. Now there is a pact to coordinate with invasions by Henry IV to destabilise Albany; there are invasions preventing the arrival of Mar's reinforcements; Mar is described as a great, competent general, whose devastated forces remained on the battlefield, totally unable to prevent Donald withdrawing, 'wearied with action'; Donald's invasion is justified as a form of forward defence to secure his conquest of Ross. But most significant of all, three hundred years after the battle, Abercromby for the first time adds to Mar's army nobles from the Spey downwards, greatly increasing the two 'locals' mentioned in the Latin accounts, Irvine of Drum and Provost Davidson. He refers to no known records to justify this detailed listing, although his inclusion of the 'Abercrombies' might suggest family knowledge (or an understandable desire to advance his forebears).

Yet the actual list of the number of important nobles and gentry *killed* is the same as in the Latin accounts, and mentions no more from the North-East other than Leslie of Balquhain and his sons.

c.1720 and c.1732. 'The privat History of the Irvins of Kingcausie since the tyme they descended from the Honorable familie of Drum Irvine', by John Irvine, 8th of Kingcausie (1664–1740)[16]

This appears in two manuscript versions, dated c.1720 and c.1732. Earlier papers, including those of John, 7th of Kingcausie, appear to have been destroyed when the house was burnt around 1680.

Anno 1410 Alexr Irvine of Drum dyed, he left of mail issew only tuo sons Alexr & John. His eldest Alexr having past his Accademik studies and being retourned from France the then dernier resort of breeding for the Young Noblmen and Gentlemen of the first rank he took the management of the estate upon him. In the litle tym after then fell out a great feud betuixt the honorable of Keith and him it grew to that pitch that the King then Ordained Drum to Mary the Lord keiths daughter under such a severe penalty that he could not refuse on purpose to take away the mistaks betuixt ye families and accordingly he maried her and brought her to Drum the nixt year being 1411 the haughty rebell Donald of the Isles had laid his plot and made to bear as he supposed he marched his tumultus armie southward as far

as Harlaw neer to Inverourey whereby the Kings comissioned
Nobility, gentry & commons are raised and did meet him at the
first place . . . before I end this combat I most return to the house
of Drum and give a short account of qt passed betuixt Drum and
his brother John . . . before he armed himslef in the Kings querele
John, asked him the Question how it cam that there was no equi-
page ordering for him, he being then a young man in his brothers
house his ansuer was they could not both risk their lives at that
tym there being no more brothers of them and he not having a
sone nor so much as ever had knouen his wife and therefor told
him he behooved to stay at hom and if it was his missfortun to
fall in the feild that he should marry his wife.

John being surprysed with both the overturs told himthat
altho he was then his parent & bound in duty to boeye him yet
he beged to be excused in both. as to the first he told him he hade
as much loyalty and personall courage as any man qt somever
and therfor could not be absent from the Kings service wtout
a reflection upon his honor, and far less could he comply in the
other shee being his [Alexander's] maried wife. Wherupon Drum
called for the preist of the parish and som other witnesses and
made it publickly knouen qt he had been privatly speaking to
his brotehr to wit that by no means wold he suffer to goe to the
camp) and If he fell that his brother should marie his wife, whom
he had never knouen whether she was man or woman for (sd
he) altho the King had full pouer to command hime any things
that was laufull I maried her yet because of ye emnmity betuixt
the family she com off and myn I have never knouen her but If
it please God to bring me back in safety from this occasion I will
instantly bed with her for now to my certain knouledge ther is
not a better woamn alive and If I retourn not then brother doe
you marie her this conferrence being ended.

So far this first manuscript illuminates the first of two famous stories
concerning Alexander Irvine of Drum: the first is his willing of his
virgin Keith wife (whom he had been forced to marry by 'the King' in
order to end a violent feud) to his reluctant brother John in the event
of his [Alexander] being killed in the forthcoming battle in order to
secure the family line, and his refusal to let his brother (here called
John) be equipped and take part in the battle.

Earlier on in this history we find the second famous story – Alexander Irvine's fatal fight with Maclean, arranged in heroic combat style by the Bishop of Aberdeen (interestingly, Harlaw lay within the Bishop's lands):

> Bishope of Aberdeen being with ye Loyall party to prevent the effusione of so much blood as was lyk to be shed in the querrell made ane overture to the Rebell that the Kings partie should make choice of one for them his partie one for him and whichever of them tuo should happen to have the advantage, his party should be esteemed victor, this proposall after much wrangling was at last embraced and the Laird of Drum was made choyce of as champion for the King and the Laird of Mcclene for the rebels . . . I retourn to the camp neer Harlaw where the two combatants formerly named wer no sooner engaged than both of them made it appear that ther pairties hade made a good choyse for they demonstrat so much courage, agility and strenth of body & limbs that it was hard for any Indefferent person (If there had been any ther) to make any conclusion upon the event till after a long and blody conflict both parties being rather wekened by loss of blood then any signs of relenting appearing it was Mcclens misfortoun to fall by Drums victorious hand and no less Drums misfortoun that one of the highland gentlemen who uas apoynted by the Rebell to be judge of Mccleans getting fair play cam first up to Drum and stabed him to the heart with a durk. The champions upon both syds being thus killed The parties engaged and the rebels wer defeted the rebelion being over and Johns murning for his brother ended he espoused the Lady Drum and by her hade three mail children that came to be men his eldest son Alexr was Laird Drum . . .

With regard to the actual battle, this is the first history to refer not merely to the nobles and gentry but also 'the commons', all raised in the cause of 'the King' – although there was no king in Scotland at the time. Donald is a mere rebel and is defeated. Was there indeed a combat between champions arranged by the Bishop of Aberdeen to prevent needless slaughter? Or was this a fanciful elevation of an incident during a savage battle? The story later arose that the families of Irvine of Drum and Hector Maclean of Duart exchanged swords thereafter at the anniversary of Harlaw, although the underhand way in which Irvine is here killed by a 'highland gentleman' might well give cause to wonder.

c.1732. This later version of the above becomes more credible:

> King Robert being then dead; the Duke of Albany being Governer sent his brother Alexander, with his Commission to raise the Nobility, Gentrie and Commons to meet and Ingadge him at the forsd place . . .
>
> . . . the parties engaged and fought so obstunately yt History relates ther wer more people of disstinction fel their, than in any batel they ever hade with forraigners. This rebellion being setled and pope John the tuentie thirds disspensation (upon the preists & other witnesses being come he espoused the Lady and by her had three sons, Alexander was Laird Drum, the second Richard of Hiltoun, the third Henry was Kingcausie . . .

A Pope John XXIII (1410–1415) did indeed reign during this period, the time of the Western Schism. The Catholic Church regards him as an antipope, but he was recognised as pope by England and France, although not, unfortunately for this history, by Scotland.[17]

c.1734. *A Brief Genealogical Account of the Family of Maclean from it's* [sic] *First Settling in the Island of Mull and Parts adjacent in the year 1390 to the year 1716,* by Hector Maclean[18]

This Clan Maclean history is based like most others of the time on an account 'Written at the desire of the Laird of MacFarlane in the year 1734 by Hector Macleane younger of Gruline in the Isle of Mull Shire of Argyle'.

> [Hector] commanded as Lieutenant General under the Earl of Ross at the battle of Harlaw in the Year 1411, where he and Irvin of Drum seeking out one another by the Armorial Bearings on their shields met and killed one another. His body was carried from the Field of Battle by the Clan Innes and Clan vic vilvory of Morvern and buried at I Collumkill [Iona].
>
> . . . After the Battle of Harlaw there was a mutual Agreement 'twixt the Lairds of Drum and MacLean to exchange swords,

which was kept up for a long Time by both Familys to cancel all
Enmity for the future that might happen on Account of the above
narrated Slaughter. Such another Agreement there was 'twixt the
Families of Grant and Maclean.

Now to the story that Irvine and Maclean slew each other in mutual
combat is added one of mutual agreement that their families should
thereafter exchange swords, 'to cancel all Enmity for the future'. We
shall see that this is developed further when examining the histories
associated with Irvine of Drum in Chapter 9.

6

The Later Eighteenth-century Accounts: Lord Forbes and His Ballad

1742. [A. Forbes] *Don: A poem*[1]

This poetical account of the battle appears as part of a long-winded and surprisingly popular poem of some 1,500 lines which describes a journey along the River Don, passing by Harlaw. Although the 1742 edition of this rambling work claimed to be a reprint of a previous 1655 edition 'with additional notes', no such earlier edition has been found and its very existence is doubted by the North-East ballad authority William Walker, who stated firmly that he 'had never seen nor heard of that edition' in his comprehensive account of *The Bards of Bon-Accords* in 1887.[2] The popular 1742 edition was reprinted many times – 1797, 1805, 1814 and 1849 – although the advertisement for the 1814 reprint warned readers that the version given in 1797 by Charles Dawson, the schoolmaster of Kemnay, had been 'mutilated, garbled and abridged . . . swelled by voluminous notes . . . at the expence of many of the most beautiful lines and passages of the poem itself'.

Even so, such was the popular demand that two versions of this 'garbled' 1797 version were also reprinted in 1805.

> Near this you'll see where famed HARLAW was fought,
> Where curst rebellion dismal mischief wrought.
> Here Doubled Donald from the isles came down,
> Stung with ambition to attack the crown:
> He, by his cunning art, and various wiles,
> Seduc'd the chieftains of the western isles:
> BROLAS, MACLACHLAN, and CARWINEN's heir,
> With brave MACLEAN, agree to risk the war,
> To aid MACDONALD, and his fate to share.

> LOCHIEL the bold, with all his martial train,
> Join and contemn the dangers of the plain.
> Here MAR resolv'd the rebel force to try,
> To tame his prowess, or attempting die.
> Great DONALD rang'd his men in armour bright,
> With shields and spears, all burning for the fight;
> Then loudly call'd to march in firm array,
> To aid each other in that doubtful day.

Donald's incursion is not only depicted simply as a wretched, ambitious rebellion against the Crown, but also in this scenario his unfortunate chiefs, including Maclean, have been 'seduced' and deceived into supporting him. Lochiel's presence is mentioned for the first time, but the others are from the writer's imagination. If the author is referring to Donald MacLean, 1st Laird of Brolas, for example, he was not born until some two hundred years later. Iain MacLachlan, Lord of Strathlachlan, was around to witness a charter in 1410, but is not recorded as having supported Donald a year later.[3] The MacLachlans of Coruanan were indeed the hereditary standard bearers to Cameron of Lochiel in Lochaber, but did not move there until 1502. Mar's force is then described:

> I see DRIMMINOR's sons rank'd on the right,
> Led by BLACK ROBERT, hateful to my sight;
> No *Lybian* lion, nor no *Greenland* bear,
> Delights so much in prey, as he in war . . .

> The GORDON troops upon the left appear;
> Them to oppose shall be our brother's care.
> Close to them join'd, I see the BISSET stand,
> With all the barons of *Strathbogy* land:
> None of more courage in the field we know,
> Who ply the sword with a more deadly blow;
> I know their blind submission to the crown,
> But this day's work shall pull their maxims down . . .
> Your fortune on your courage must rely,
> A shameful death attends us if we fly.

> From *Aberdeen* five hundred warriors came,
> All clad in steel, and not unknown to fame:

Their provost DAV'DSON led the chosen band,
And brave HUGH ROSE next him had the command:
Both men of prowess and superior force;
One led the foot, the other rul'd the horse.
The gallant FRASER, baron of *Philorth*,
Of well know courage and undoubted worth,
With KEITHs and FORBESES, in bright array . . .
ANGUS' high sheriff join'd them, with the rest
Of AIRLY's sons, in manly armour drest.
MAR led the centre close, his wings at large,
Advancing keen, in order, to the charge.
The noble KEITH join'd ROBERT in the van,
Who led the friends and followers of the clan.
DRUM, with the LEITHs and LESLIES of *Balquhoin,*
Upon the left the gallant GORDONS join . . .

The author is clearly a Forbes family aficionado, although if the 'Black Robert' he detests so much refers to Sir John de Forbes, Lord of Forbes, called 'Sir John of the Black Lip', he died around 1405.[4] Otherwise it is Keith and his followers who lead the vanguard, with Leiths, Leslies and Gordons on the left wing. The Sheriff of Angus this time leads no wing. Aberdeen's contribution of some thirty burgesses has been enlarged twelve-fold to consist of five hundred armoured warriors, both foot soldiers and cavalry. This begins to cast considerable doubt on the poem's veracity. No Hugh Rose appears on the list in the Aberdeen Council Register of the burgesses who were 'chosen to go out against the katerans'.

First KEITH and FORBES to the battle flew,
The brave example all the rest pursue.
Here, like rapacious wolves, the foes engage,
Scots rush on *Scots*, and all was blood and rage.
The brave MACLEAN fought on MACDONALD's right,
And like the mountain bear maintain'd the fight:
Though sorely wounded, press'd, and bath'd in blood,
He kept his ground and made the party good . . .
At last the LESLIES bord'ring on the DON,
Fir'd by the chief who led the warriors on,
First pierc'd the ranks and broke McDONALD's horse,

And taught the foes to own superior force.
The DRUM's proud baron, on a dapple grey,
Spoke to the KEITH, and pointed out the prey . . .
And rushing forward, with a well-aim'd thrust,
DRUM stretch'd the gallant hero in the dust.
His men sore vex'd to see their ranks o'erthrown,
Grieve for their master's loss more than their own.
BROLAS enrag'd, calls outaloud to all,
'Revenge MACLEAN, or bravely by him fall': . . .
The yielding islanders his presence turns,
He rushes where the battle fiercest burns:
MACLACHLAN and CARWINEN fresh pursue,
And kindle all the rage of war anew . . .
Nine of the bravest LESLIES press'd the plain,
And round the warriors lay whole crowds of slain.
GORDONS and FORBESES promiscuous fall,
Death and destruction seem to threaten all . . .
Great DONALD when he saw MACLEAN was lost,
The pride, the strength, the bulwark of his host . . .
DAV'DSON he slew, and brave HUGH ROSE bore back,
And thousands perish'd in this fierce attack . . .
The gallant FRASER here resign'd his breath,
And crown'd with glory, evem smil'd in death .
Tumbling in dust, heroes on heroes lay,
And in sad anguish sobb'd their souls away.
All round the field, the bravest warriers bleed,
And hopes and fears alternately succeed;
Till KEITH call'd ROBERT, and was heard to say,
'Ourselves must force these rebels to give way.'

Amidst the intensity and savagery of the battle, Irvine of Drum, in this version on horseback, now spears Maclean – 'a gallant hero', instead of engaging him in famed mortal combat on foot. The bravery of the Leslies gets them slaughtered by the imagined Highland chiefs, along with the Gordons and the Forbeses. In the following lines 'Black Robert' eventually leads the charges that force the Highlanders to begin to flee, Donald included. Lochiel rampages in Donald's defence and 'Black Robert' bears down on him, to challenge 'his former friend' with such entreaties as:

'What brought thee here to this detested war,
Against thy king, a rebel's fate to share!

To get a remarkably chivalric response:

'Thy vile reproaches ill become the brave:
I live thy friend, yet scorn to be thy slave . . .
But since MACDONALD flies to save his life,
Our quarrel ends, and needless were our strife.
To thee and fate I yield' – He grumbling said,
And, frowning, sheath'd his unavailing blade.
Quick jumping from his horse, the hero ran,
With outstretch'd arms, to meet the gallant man:
The chief and hero all their rage resigned,
And sacred friendship fills each noble mind.
Then all submitted to the victor's will,
No dastard should durst more attempt to kill:
The royal pardon soon ran o'er the plain
And all the rage of war was hush'd again.

Thus noble chivalry ends the day. All the invaders yield, disdaining to flee, and are granted a royal pardon on the spot. It is not surprising that this splendid farrago was republished so often by popular request, and although it appears to contain little of historical value and much misinformation and sheer fancy, it must have been influential in forming the 'popular history' of the region, despite the fact that 'it agrees with neither name or date' especially regarding the Forbes family.[5]

It should be said, though, that in his 1797 footnotes, Dawson does give the first mention of the story that Alexander Irvine of Drum, on the way to the battle in which he is to die, 'made his testament' at the 'Drum Stone', 'in sight of Drum and Harlaw'. Dawson makes no mention, however, of the two other later legends about Irvine: that he fell in mutual combat with Maclean; and that he requested, if he died in the battle, that his brother Robert should marry Irvine's widow, the marriage so far being unconsummated. These stories will only appear in much later accounts.

Otherwise the poem cannot be regarded as having any historical value.

1784. 'Memoirs of the House of Forbes', by J. Forbes[6]

This bound manuscript in Castle Forbes is dated 1784. It does, however, refer to a cardinal, who died in 1741, as being still alive, although as this cleric was of the French branch of the Forbes, news of his death may not have arrived by the time the 'Memoirs' were written.[7] As well as genealogies, it offers 'Candid and unbyased Accounts of the Lives & Actions of the most Famous and Illustrious Heros of that Name ... since the Dayes of Bruce and Ballioll with curious Occurrences'. Perhaps unsurprisingly, these memoirs describe not just the Battle of Harlaw but a crucial role in it for Forbes.

The 'Memoirs' follow mainly Boece/Bellenden in describing the situation of young Euphemia Ross, including Donald's marriage to her aunt, but also they repeat the Sleat historian's rumour that the young woman was manipulated, and adding that she was perhaps even murdered by the Governor Albany in order to obtain her Earldom for his son. There is no mention of the story that Albany insultingly provoked Donald, nor that Donald made his claim and his move on hearing that Euphemia had entered a nunnery, and was thus dead in a legal sense. But although the 'Memoirs' agree that Donald was the 'undoubted heir', they do not accept the violence with which he set about claiming it.

The Lord of the Isles' first move is to bring over an extremely large army (still reckoned at ten thousand men) with which he is able to occupy Ross easily, a doubly satisfactory outcome in that its people welcome him back as their 'just' lord and master. They confirm Buchanan's belief that this warm reception deluded Donald into further action:

> Donald thus flusht with success, stops not here, but is emboldened to attempt greater matters (his mind being set upon plunder and pillage of the Country) he passes over into Murray, barbarously harasses the whole land, and thence proceeds forewards in his depredations into Strathbogie, and from thence to Garioch, intending to burn and pillage the city of Aberdeen.
>
> To stop this Current [courant] (the greatness & proprinquity of the danger not admitting delayes) Alexander Stuart E[arl] of Mar and natural Son of Alex[ande]r E[arl] of Buchan the Governors brother, and third son of King Robert the 2nd, followed by

the most of the Nobility benorth Tay, having chosen him their Generall encounters Donald at a litle village in Garioch called Harlaw and joyns battle. The fight continued long and was extraordinary bloody, the Nobility and Gentry, who were with the Earle contending for glory and honour as well as life against the cruetly [sic] and barbarisme of the opposite party, In a word they fought it out till night did part them; so that it may be truly said, that they were both rather wearied with fighting, than that either party had the better, which made the event of the fight so uncertain, y[e]t when both sides began to reckon up how many they had lost neither could pretend to an indisputed victory.

In this battle there fell so many eminent and Noble personages as scarce ever perished in one fight against a foreign enemy for many years before. Of the Islanders 900 were slain with McGillan & Mackintoish two of their principale chieftaines next to Donald. Of the other part many Angus Gentlemen, the Lo[rd] Ogilvie, a Nobleman of singular goodness and approved valour, Scrimgeor Constable of Dundee a bold and daring Man Alexander Irvine Laird of Drum, for his great strength and courage famous to posterity Robert Maule of Panmuir Thomas Murray, Abernethie of Saltoun, Alex[ande]r Straitoun, the valiant Laird of Lauriston, Robert Davidson provest of Aberdeen all knights with many other Barons & Gentlemen, among others eleven sons of that Laird of of [sic] Balquhain, of whom we just now spoke dyed there in the bed of Honour.

Donald leaving the Victory to his Enemies travells all night flying to Ross, and from thence to the Isles, was shortly after reconciled to the Governour/ it was fought in the year 1411, To which the famous University of St Andrews owes its rise.

The 'Memoirs' confirm that neither side claimed a victory, but describe major losses following a long and 'extraordinary bloody' fight to a standstill. The death toll amongst Donald's forces rises from the hundred and eighty of the Sleat historian to the nine hundred also given by Bower, Mair and Boece. As with those Latin chroniclers, the listing of slain nobles includes Irvine of Drum and Provost Davidson from the North-East, although this time Andrew Leslie of Balquhain and his sons also make an appearance. The principal addition, however, to the heroic North-East combatants is – 'Lord Forbes':

It was at this Battle that Alexander Lord Forbes left many honorable marks of his courage and bravery, and did such astonishing feats in armes as mightily endeared him to the Generall, who entertained such an extraordinary esteem of him, That he entred into a noble friendship, sympathy and affection and agreeablness of humour and disposition, together with their constant and inseperable society so strictly cementing it, that it continued indissoluble until the Earles Death.

This is the first time that 'Lord Forbes' is described as being at the actual battle, fighting so well and valiantly that he was to earn the Earl of Mar's undying gratitude.

At this point, therefore, it is worth considering the famous 'Forbes' Harlaw ballad. Its aim is not just to celebrate the above undoubted prowess of Lord Forbes in securing a complete victory, but also to portray him and a brother as the only heroes of the conflict. The Earl of Mar and all the other knights and nobles are nowhere to be seen. It is sung to this day, especially by Travellers, and is regarded by them and many others as the genuine traditional ballad, composed around the time of the battle.

'The Battle of Harlaw' (Child 163)[8]

Professor Francis James Child of Harvard assembled, categorised, numbered. and published his monumental *English and Scottish Popular Ballads* between 1882 and 1898, and these 'story' ballads have since been designated by their numbers in that publication. Child, however, only found two versions of a ballad called 'The Battle of Harlaw' (Child 163). His best, A-text, of twenty-five stanzas was collected from 'country people' by Charles Elphinstone Dalrymple of Kinaldie in Aberdeenshire, and his brother, around 1838. Furthermore, Child's lesser, B-text consisted only of three verses taken from a version printed in 1823 in *The Thistle of Scotland* by Alexander Laing, an Aberdeen printer and chapman. Indeed Laing himself thought the three verses were quite sufficient to demonstrate that 'The Battle of Harlaw' was merely 'a burlesque song sung in the country . . . I think it not worth the attention of the public.'[9]

David Buchan, though, considered that the ballad had indeed been composed 'near 1411', and was the version mentioned in the *Complaynt of Scotland*; he believed that the reason the ballad showed few variants (if many are present they are taken to be a sign of a long-standing composition) was that Laing had actually collected a full version of it, which he had then hawked as a single-sheet round Aberdeenshire.[10] No such printed sheet has been identified.

The Greig-Duncan Folk Song Collection, however, amassed by a North-East schoolmaster, Gavin Greig, and a minister, the Reverend James Bruce Duncan, in the decade before the Great War of 1914–18, has sixteen examples of the long 'Forbes' version.[11] As Greig pointed out, this was the only Harlaw ballad still in existence in his time, and *he* firmly considered it to be 'a genuine ballad of Harlaw, sung to a genuine folk-tune in the true traditional way'.[12]

The following ballad text is a compilation of representative stanzas taken from versions provided by Greig and Duncan's informants. The repeated choruses are not given; they were presumably intended to imitate the sound of bagpipes ('Wi' my dirrum du, dirrum du/Daddie dirrum day').

> As I cam in by Dunnideer
> And doon by Netherha'
> There were fifty thousand redcoats
> A' marchin tae Harlaw.

This opening stanza alone raises three matters of concern. 'Red coats' were not worn by any British force before Cromwell's New Model Army in 1645. Buchan felt that 'the folk had conflated two incursions of Highlandmen more than three hundred years apart' and that the ballad's 'disengagement' reflected the 'comparatively passive' attitude, and 'objectivity' of the North-Easterners to the 1745 Jacobite incursion.[13] But in fact the Jacobite and Episcopal North-East of Scotland was heavily engaged in the Rebellion, fighting off an invasion of Government-supporting Highlanders at Inverurie, and providing considerable forces for the Jacobite cause that departed to take part in the Battle of Culloden in 1746. Moreover, the crucial tactics which helped win Culloden were rehearsed in Aberdeen by the fifteen full Government regiments which then occupied the city until February 1747.[14]

Donald's army would not have come in past the ruined fortress of Dunnideer and by the Hill of Netherhall. This would have involved both coming south from Huntly via the Rhynie Gap, slap into Forbes' defences, then having to get past the castle of the belligerent Sir Andrew Leslie of Balquhain, ready to throw all his fighting sons into any battle, before eventually attempting to cross and re-cross the Urie river and its flood plain before hauling up on to the plateau of Harlaw. The army came further north along the King's Highway from Huntly via the Glens of Foudland.

Fifty thousand, furthermore, is a considerable exaggeration of their numbers, which the chroniclers, Bower, Mair and Buchanan, all give as the same precise figure for Donald's army – ten thousand at the most – though Boece did state simply that Donald had brought an 'enormous' host (*ingenti*).

Nevertheless, it makes for a gripping opening verse from the Lowland observer of a ballad composed, unusually, in Scots:[15]

> As I cam in and further on
> And doon and by Balquhain
> It's there I met Sir James the Rose
> Wi' him Sir John the Graeme.

Sweeping close past the fortress of Balquhain with its belligerent castellan Andrew Leslie, and his formidable twelve (legitimate) sons, at least six (and perhaps eleven) of whom were to fall in the coming battle, would indeed have been a serious error, and one Donald certainly avoided by coming further north by the Glens of Foudland.[16]

What of Sir James the Rose and Sir John the Graeme? Child refers to an early version of their ballad mentioned in Motherwell Manuscripts written in 1825 and after, and occurring in 'early stall prints' and 'from the recitations of elderly people'. Three verses of it are quoted by Greig in his *Buchan Observer* article of 25 August 1908, entitled 'Sir James the Rose. A Historical Ballad', but he goes on to say: 'Sir James the Rose . . . The version now generally known and sung . . . is credited to Michael Bruce (1746–1767)'.[17] Although this is a lengthy ballad, it is not of any quality. For example, the following verse:

> Behind him basely came the Graeme
> And pierced him [Sir James] in the side
> Out spouting came the purple stream
> And all his tartans dyed.[18]

Thus these two gentlemen appear to have been brought in simply to provide additional colour from another ballad, in which they are in fact mortal enemies, and one which was not composed until after 1760. (In that ballad, Sir James' family territory is given as Skye 'where my brave brothers bide'. This *may* have been a reason he became associated with this 'Forbes' ballad, which also mistakenly depicts Donald as coming from that island.) Despite being on the other side of the hills from the invaders, the singer now feels able to interrogate them; they reply in comic, pseudo-Highland speech:

> Oh came ye frae the Hielands, man
> Oh cam ye a' the wey?
> Saw ye McDonald and his men
> As they cam in frae Skye?
>
> Yes we cam frae the Highlands
> An' we cam a' the wey
> And saw McDonald and his men
> As they cam in frae Skye.
>
> Oh was ye near McDonell's men?
> Did ye their numbers see?
> Come, tell me Johnnie Hielanman
> What micht their numbers be?
>
> Me pe very near to them
> Yes me their numbers spy
> There be ninety thousand Highlanders
> As they cam frae the Skye.

After his death, Somerled's territories were split up using the Norse system. When the Hebrides were ceded by Norway to Scotland in 1266, Skye and Lewis were given to the Earldom of Ross, Islay to the Macdonalds, Uist to MacRuari; and Mull to MacDougall.[19] So although Donald and his men are depicted as coming from Skye, that is one territory Donald did not own, and had not come from. Along with Lewis, it belonged to the Earldom of Ross, which he was trying to wrest from the Albany Stewarts. By the time of this composition, however, Skye would indeed have become Macdonald territory, again highlighting its late date.[20]

The burlesque of Highland attempts at Lowland speech is even more pronounced in other versions of the ballad: 'Yes, I pe fae the Highlands cam/Yes, me cam a' the wye'.[21] Buchan considered that this mockery reflected a post-1745 stage in Highland/North-East relations, when the Highlander had become 'a rather comic fellow, wild yet courteous, proud yet naïve, whose comic side became very pronounced when he tried to grapple with the foreign tongue of Lowland Scots'.[22] William Donaldson, on the other hand, painted a different picture of the once feared Highlander having been transformed into a heroic figure, the 'Bonny Highland Laddie', and at a much later date than the time of the battle.[23] Habitués of the English court, Donald and his senior officers would have had good English (not to mention the Latin necessary for a lengthy sojourn at Oxford that Richard II offered him).[24] His army (as well as many on the 'Lowland' side) would have been speaking a form of Gaelic.[25]

> 'If this be true' says John the Graeme
> 'We'll sheath our swords wi speed
> We'll call upon our merry men
> And lightly mount our steed.'
>
> 'Oh no, oh no' says James the Rose
> 'No, that mauna be
> The Rose's clan was never beat
> We'll try what we can dee.'

The above two verses may be discounted, for both John and James are intruders from another late ballad.

> As I cam on, an farther on,
> An doun an by Harlaw,
> They fell fu' close on ilka side;
> Sic strokes ye never saw.
>
> They fell fu' close on ilka side,
> Sic strokes ye never saw;
> For ilka sword gave clash for clash,
> At the battle o' Harlaw.
>
> The Hielanmen, wi their lang swords,
> They laid on us fu' sair,

> And they drove back our merry men
> Three acres breadth an mair.

According to the chroniclers, Donald's forces, encamped on the plateau of Harlaw, were precipitously attacked by the Earl of Mar's army, before all reinforcements had appeared. Reinforcements that were flung in completely disorganised. Mar appears to have broken a principal rule of medieval warfare: 'Never attack first', for he is described as losing control of his force, with great and unnecessary loss of life – as indeed the French were to experience at Agincourt four years later. None of the chroniclers make mention of a heavy reverse of Mar's forces, although it was not unlikely; the 'Highland charge' was to prove devastating until Culloden.[26]

The 'lang sword' – the two-handed claymore – does come into use from around 1400 onwards. (The 'claymore' of popular Romantic image – a basket-hilted, single-handed sword, still in modern regimental use – is a very much later weapon.)

> Lord Forbes to his brother said
> 'It's brother don't you see
> They kill our men on every side
> And we'll be forced to flee.'
>
> 'Oh no, oh no' my brother dear
> Oh no, that maunna be
> Ye'll take your broad sword in your hand
> And go the ranks with me.'

With these verses, the ballad's celebration of 'Lord Forbes' and a brother as the *only* Lowland heroes of the battle, begins. (Forbes' youngest brother, Alaster Cam, would seem a suitable candidate; he was already famed for winning his lands of Brux in single combat in 1409.)[27]

> Lord Forbès to his men did say
> 'Ye'll take your breaths awhile
> Till I do send my servant
> It's for my coat of mail.'
>
> His servant to Drumminor rode
> His horse he didna fail
> For in two oors and a quarter
> He brought his coat of mail

Douglas Simpson felt that Forbes, once he knew that Donald was approaching via the King's Highway from Huntly, through the Garioch towards Inverurie, would have been able to leave his defensive positions and hurry over to the battle.[28] But without his armour? As noted earlier, the Forbes family 'Memoirs' maintain that Alexander Forbes (who was soon to be made the premier baron of Scotland) *did* play a crucial role in the outcome of the battle, for which Mar was forever grateful, but was this by arriving at the battle, amongst the later disorganised and piecemeal reinforcements described by Boece, or by holding the crucial Rhynie Gap and the Glen of Brux, thus preventing Donald making a southern and then eastern attack on Aberdeen? Although 'mail' is appropriate armour for the period, and the timing is close to that which would have taken a round trip of thirty miles, that such a knight would have omitted to bring his armour to a major battle in the first place is, to say the least, unlikely.[29]

In fact, in 1411, no 'Lord Forbes' existed. Sir Alexander, Laird of Forbes, son of Sir John Forbes of the Black Lip, was not made a Lord of Parliament as 'Lord Forbes' until some thirty years later.[30] It was not until 1440 that an earlier earth and timber Castle Forbes was abandoned for a site a mile and a half to its south, where the tower of Druminnor, 'a major stone building', was begun.[31]

> Then back to back brothers twa
> Gaed in amang the throng
> They laid them doon the Hielandmen
> Wi' swords baith sharp and long.
>
> Lord Forbes being young and stoot
> Put on his coat o' mail
> And he charged Macdonald through the ranks
> To fight wi' him himsel.
>
> The first ae stroke that Forbes struck
> He gart McDonald reel
> And the neist ae stroke that Forbes struck
> The brave McDonald fell.

Born around 1380, Forbes was in his thirties (his 'stoutness' will refer to his great, dependable bravery, not his waist), only half the age of Donald, whom he is now credited with slaying in single combat, despite the fact that the Lord of the Isles survived the battle to die at

his castle of Ardtornish, in Morvern, in 1423.[32] No other heroes are to
be seen, not even the Earl of Mar.

> But when they saw their chief was gone
> They fought fu' lion-like.
> But Lord Forbes wi' his wyty sword
> He garred them fidge and fyke.   [jerk about]

> When they saw their chief was deid
> Wi' him they ran awa
> And buried him at Leggat's den
> A lairge mile frae Harlaw.

> Some rade, some ran, and some did gang,
> They were o' sma record;
> But Forbes an his merry men,
> They slew them a' the road.

Mair states that Donald was forced into a fighting retreat (but not
routed). All that is known of the actual end of the battle is Boece's
account that it was fought to a standstill, its outcome was undecided,
and at nightfall both sides 'retreated to the nearby hills'.

> On Munonday at morning
> The battle it began
> On Saturday at gloamin'
> Ye'd scarce tell wha had won.

> And sic a weary burying
> The like ye never saw
> As was the Sunday after that,
> On the muirs down by Harlaw.

> Gin oniebody spier at you
> For them that is awa
> Ye'll tell them plain and very plain
> 'They're sleepin' at Harlaw.'

The battle lasted only one Friday, not almost a week. The ballad, however, for once is accurate – in describing the uncertainty of the result.
Aberdeen University's Librarian, Douglas Simpson, an authority on
the history of the region, especially its castles, also described the
finding of a mass grave in 1837, but north of the battlefield itself.[33]

The Maitlands of Balhalgardy have ploughed the plateau since before the battle and for the six hundred years thereafter, but have done so without turning up any further graves. Was it indeed the case that any bodies not carried away were buried 'in the moors beneath', as recounted in this ballad?

The evidence, therefore, is that this largely inaccurate but entertainingly spirited ballad, clearly by a Forbes family supporter, was not in existence before the latter half of the eighteenth century. Simpson, nevertheless, did feel that some of the verses – such as those referring to the 'lang swords' of Donald's men – were echoes of accounts from the past.[34] Buchan believed that, despite the many anomalies, this ballad was both the original mentioned in *The Complaynt of Scotland* of c.1550 and of value historically.[35] He suggested that the mention of 'Redcoats' as defenders was a confusion with the 1745 Rebellion caused by a process in which an original 1411 ballad had segued into one in which 'the folk imagination reacted to, moulded, and used for its own emotional purposes, the raw material of the historical event'. Hamish Henderson thought that Buchan's 'new look' at the ballad, though 'clear-sighted', raised more questions than it answered, and felt that the above Battle of Inverurie should have been considered as a source for such anachronisms, forgetting that there would have been few, if any, Redcoats in the Inverurie fight, which was between the Highland Independent Companies, led by Norman MacLeod of MacLeod, on the Government side, with Lord Lewis Gordon defending Aberdeenshire for the Jacobites. [36]

Nevertheless, there has been a general consensus, especially amongst Child's informants, that this 'Forbes' ballad was relatively modern.[37] Alexander Keith considered that it was 'comparatively recent' because of the 'distinct and unusual correspondence of stanza with stanza', i.e. it lacked the variants that an old ballad generates with the passage of time.[38] Even modern Traveller versions show no such variation.[39] Charles Dalrymple (1817–1891) even suggested that such variants as there were might well have been induced by editors such as Lady Jane Scott, and indeed by himself, for in 1888 he confessed to having made changes to the ballad in his 'youthful self-sufficiency' some fifty years before. [40]

Buchan had also supported Douglas Simpson's suggestion that Forbes did eventually arrive at the battle, citing the evidence of two

Harlaw plateau from the west. The Monument erected in 1914 in the distance.

Harlaw battlefield. Harlaw House in distance.

Donald's approach from the north-west. Monument in the distance.

The ruined castle of the Leslies of Balquhain.

David Irvine, 26th Baron of Drum, before the thirteenth-century Tower of Drum.

The Drum Stone.

Lord Provost Stephen of Aberdeen and Robert Maitland of Balhalgardy at the 600th anniversary of the battle.

The Harlaw Monument with Bennachie in the south-west.

twentieth-century authors (who themselves gave no sources) that this was a firm Forbes family belief.[41] As already noted, the 'Memoirs of the House of Forbes' do in fact claim that Forbes was present, and indeed displayed such remarkable bravery and astonishing feats of arms that he earned the undying friendship of the Earl of Mar. They are dated 1784, which is around the time this ballad was composed. What is interesting, however, is that their author ignored (or was unaware of) any details given by the mediaeval chroniclers, or even by the seventeenth or eighteenth-century writers, although he may have been aware of the avowal in the actual 'Memoirs' that Lord Forbes *was* at the battle. The ballad is thus strewn with historical errors and seemingly provides no reliable historical evidence, other than, of course,

'Ye'd scarce tell wha had won.'

Wondering why, post-Culloden, it was thought valuable or even necessary to portray Lord Forbes and a brother as the sole defenders of Lowland Scotland against a huge horde of savage Highlanders leads into the uncertain realm of historical speculation. During the 1745/6 Jacobite Rising, Duncan Forbes of Culloden had strongly supported the Government side, becoming lord advocate, and later proposing the establishment of Highland regiments. He was personally responsible for ensuring that many of the most powerful Highland chiefs did not join Charles' campaign, and appealed afterwards for lenient treatment of the rebels.

Over in the North-East, however, Alexander Forbes, 4th Lord Pitsligo, although from a Whig family, took part in the Jacobite Risings of both 1715 and 1745. His estates were forfeited but he managed to hide on his own lands until his death in 1762. If the ballad was intended to help restore his family's fortunes (and perhaps portray it as a bulwark against incursions of 'Wild Scots' from the west), it was unsuccessful, for on the death of his son the title became dormant.[42]

Nevertheless, it is inconceivable that Forbes' contribution to the outcome of the Battle of Harlaw was not crucial. Not only did his array of fortifications block any attempt by Donald to take the old southern then eastern route to Aberdeen, but the very threat of their existence 'herded' him along the Huntly–Inverurie–Aberdeen King's Highway where Mar's force could be waiting in forward defence. Furthermore, at any time Forbes' forces had the potential to sweep up through the

Rhynie Gap and cut off or harass Donald's return from Harlaw. It is not surprising, therefore, that Donald decided to withdraw very rapidly in the six hours of darkness that were available to him during the night following the battle, in order to bypass this threat. The mystery remains – where, and at what point did Forbes display his great bravery in actual fighting that so impressed the Earl of Mar?

For despite its general historical inaccuracy, the eighteenth-century 'Forbes ballad' does serve to highlight another historical puzzle – why the Latin chroniclers named no North-East nobles being at the Battle of Harlaw other than Irvine of Drum. Irvine, admittedly, had long been a close associate of Mar's, especially on his Continental exploits, but so had Leslie of Balquhain, who is not mentioned as having taken part until Abercromby's history and the above 'Memoirs' were written, with both Irvine and Leslie 'continuing as his regular councillers [sic] for three decades.'[43]

Furthermore, Mar's closest ties within Aberdeenshire remained with the Forbes family and both earl and kindred benefited from this bond. It was surely no coincidence that the four sons of John Forbes ['of the Black Lip'] (who died in 1406) all received advantageous marriages and extensive grants of land during Alexander Stewart's years of dominance in the region.

This splendid eighteenth-century ballad is indeed fabulous, but if we turn now to the nineteenth and twentieth-century visions it will be to enter the realm of even greater speculation.

7

The Early Nineteenth-century Accounts

F our hundred and more years have now passed since the day of the battle and accounts must now be treated with even more caution, even those written by North-East historians.

1816. *The Antiquary,* by Sir Walter Scott[1]

Perhaps the most famous stanzas regarding the Battle of Harlaw appear in Walter Scott's *The Antiquary*, published in 1816, but supposedly set in 1794. It is part of the swansong of an old woman, Elspeth Cheyne of Craigburnfoot, who confuses Harlaw with a 1715 battle, for she claims to be 'the daughter of that Reginald Cheyne who died to save his master, Lord Glenallan, on the field of Sheriffmuir'. Although it did not become a song, it is probably the most quoted poetic account of the battle:

Now haud your tongue, baith wife and carle,
And listen, great and sma',
And I will sing of Glenallan's Earl
That fought on the red Harlaw.

The cronach's cried on Bennachie,
And doun the Don and a',
And hieland and lawland may mournfu' be
For the sair field of Harlaw.

Scott appeals to those who see Scottish history as a romantic running battle between 'Highland' and 'Lowland', a contest only ending with Culloden. Indeed, in his notes to *The Antiquary* he stated that 'The great battle of Harlaw ... might be said to determine whether the Gaelic or Saxon race should be predominant in Scotland'. With Gaelic at this time a tongue heard as far east as Fife, it was a language of both Donald's and Mar's troops and it is doubtful if everyone in 1411 would have seen Scotland and its peoples that way.

While Donald certainly came from the Norse-Gael stock of Somerled, his cousin the Earl of Mar, who was reputedly raised in the Highlands by his Gaelic-speaking mother and in his early days followed as violent a career as his father, the Wolf of Badenoch, was hardly a 'Saxon' nobleman. Although Alexander Stewart gained the Lordship of Mar though marriage to Countess Isabella, whose husband, Sir Malcolm Drummond, Lord of Mar, was murdered in 1402, the traditional view has been that Alexander was complicit in the murder, that he assailed and captured the countess's castle of Kildrummy, and that he subsequently forced Isabella to marry him.[2] This interpretation has been questioned in recent years by historians who ascribe his remarkable ascent to the rising political fortunes of his father, the Earl of Buchan, and to the support of prominent local families, who welcomed the protection Alexander offered against raids from the west.[3] As a matter of fact, Bower seems to be the only source describing Mar in his youth as being 'headstrong and wild', the 'leader of a band of caterans'.[4]

> If they hae twenty thousand blades,
> And we twice ten times ten,
> Yet they hae but their tartan plaids,
> And we are mail-clad men.
>
> My horse shall ride through ranks sae rude,
> As through the moorland fern,
> Then neer let the gentle Norman blude
> Grow cauld for Highland kerne.

Whether or not any of Mar's followers would have seen themselves as Normans three centuries after they were first introduced to Scotland is a moot point, but it (almost) suits Scott's depiction of the battle as a death-struggle between Celts and Saxons for the control of Scottish civilisation.[5] As the pressure from the Norsemen had earlier forced those Celts who had colonised Dalriada from Ireland eastwards to merge with the Picts, it is ironic that Mar's soldiers may have possessed as many Celtic genes as Donald's 'Norse-Gaels'.[6] The reference to 'gentle Norman blude', however, was quite a change from Scott's vigorous promotion of Britain's true origin being from the noble Anglo-Saxons (subdued by brutal Normans) he portrayed in his *Ivanhoe* (1819). His revisionism is perhaps understandable in a period during which France was Britain's prime enemy.

Scott does seem to be familiar with some of the mediaeval chroniclers' accounts, even if he doubles their estimate of Donald's forces. He appears also to have accepted Boece's description of Mar's tactical errors, for his *Antiquary* character Cheyne, 'blamed himself for the counsel he gave "to fight befoe Mar came up wi' Mearns, and Aberdeen, and Angus"'. His portrayal of Highlanders as a wild and barbarous people, fit only to be cut down by superior Teuton knights, seems far from his sensitive depiction of them two years previously in *Waverley* (1814).

1819. *The Caledonian Itinerary,* by Alexander Laing[7]

Alexander Laing (1778–1838) was born at Coull in Aberdeenshire, and followed a varied career, including itinerant bookseller and stationer, as well as editor of annuals such as *The Eccentric Magazine*. He published *Scarce Ancient Ballads Never before Published with Notes* in 1822, and a similar collection, *The Thistle of Scotland*, the following year. His chief work was a useful collection of folklore, *The Donean Tourist, Interspersed with Anecdotes and Ancient Ballads*, published in 1828, establishing him as an antiquarian, but an Aberdeen publication referring to Harlaw, however briefly, was his first attempt, with the self-explanatory title, *The Caledonian Itinerary, or, A Tour on the Banks of the Dee: A Poem with historical notes from the best authorities*. It reads as follows:

> In 1411, when Donald essayed to seize the helm of Scotland, and mount the royal chair, to aid his plan, he collected an army composed of chiefs of the clans, viz Carwinens, Camerons, McIntoshes, McKechnies, McLauchlans, McKays and McLeans, and marched to Harlaw. Stuart, Earl of Mar, headed the royalists, aided by the Gordons and the Forbeses, and marched to give him battle. Here the fight commenced with keenness, but the Stuarts were victorious. Donald lost 900 men, his baggage and ammunition; and his standard was born to Aberdeen by Provost Davidson, as a trophy of victory. In 1416, Stuart agreed with the Lords, and entered into a treaty to liberate the King.

Even though Laing's 'best authorities' for the above were '*Dawson's Don Poem*' and '*Abercrombie's Mart. Ach, vol 3*', his account of Harlaw borders on the imaginary throughout. Unusually for a Lowland historian, he claims to detail the clans accompanying Donald – including the likes of the Mackays whom Donald had in fact to defeat in order to occupy Ross. That Donald lost nine hundred men is in agreement with other historians, but his army would have travelled fast and light, and possessing no weapons requiring 'ammunition'.

Donald definitely loses the battle, though, and Provost Davidson (although actually he is dead) is credited with taking Donald's banner to Aberdeen. On Mar's side, the Gordons, and the Forbeses are once more given sole credit for being his supporters. Amongst so many inaccuracies, it is difficult to accept Laing's firm opinion that Donald was aiming for the throne of Scotland, and not merely the Earldom of Ross.

Although his itinerary was avidly subscribed to by many collectors, it is important not to confuse him with the learned bibliophile and librarian, David Laing (1793–1878) whose passion for Scottish history resulted in many scholarly editions. He published a version of the 'Ramsay' Harlaw ballad and briefly discussed its 'considerable antiquity' in his 1826 *Early Metrical Tales*.[8]

1828. *Tales of a Grandfather*, by Sir Walter Scott[9]

Scott's mention of the battle in his *Tales* may be brief, but his relief that it prevented Highland barbarians from overrunning Scotland is considerable:

> One of the most remarkable events during his [Governor Albany] government was the battle of Harlaw. This was fought by a prince, called Donald of the Isles, who possessed all the islands on the west side of Scotland. He was also the proprietor of great estates on the mainland, and aspired to the rank, and used the style, of an independent sovereign.
>
> This Donald, in the year 1411, laid claim to the earldom of Ross, then vacant, which the Regent had determined to bestow on a member of his own family. Donald of the Isles raised ten thousand men, all Highlanders like himself, and invading the north of Scotland, came as far as a place called Harlaw, about ten miles from Aberdeen. Here he was encountered by the Earl of

Mar, at the head of an inferior army, but composed of Lowland gentlemen, better armed and disciplined than the followers of Donald. A most desperate battle ensued, in which both parties suffered great loss. On that of Donald, the chiefs of the clans called MacIntosh and Maclean were both slain, with about a thousand men. Mar lost nearly five hundred brave gentlemen, amongst them Ogilvy, Scrymgeour, Irvine of Drum and other men of rank.

The Provost of Aberdeen, who had brought to the Earl of Mar's host a detachment of the inhabitants of that city, was slain, fighting bravely. This loss was so much regretted by the citizens that a resolution was adopted, that no Provost should in future go out in his official capacity beyond the limits of the immediate territory of the town. This rule is still observed.

But though the Lowlanders suffered severely the Highlanders had the worst, and were obliged to retreat after the battle. This was fortunate for Scotland, since otherwise the Highlanders, at that time a wild and barbarous people, would have overrun, and perhaps actually conquered, a great part of the civilised country. The battle of Harlaw was long remembered, owing to the bravery with which the field was disputed, and the numbers which fell on both sides.

Scott does seem to be familiar with some of the mediaeval chroniclers' accounts, including numbers of the slain, and he includes their mention of Ogilvy, Scrymgeour and Provost Davidson, and similarly omits the North-East nobility other than Irvine of Drum. As noted, he appears to have accepted Boece's description of Mar's tactical errors, for his earlier *Antiquary* character Cheyne, 'blamed himself for the counsel he gave "to fight befoe Mar came up wi' Mearns, and Aberdeen, and Angus"'. Interestingly, his only footnote is to his protégé Tytler's as yet unpublished *History*. The fable about the future town-bound Provosts is recounted.

He describes Donald as a prince in his own kingdom, capable of conquering a great part of Scotland. Unlike the Latin chroniclers, Scott says he was 'obliged' to retreat, but also depicts the brave determination shown by both sides in the battle, together with the great loss of lives. Most importantly, he depicts the Highlanders as 'wild and barbarous', ready to over-run 'civilised' Scotland.

1829. *History of Scotland,* by Patrick Tytler[10]

Patrick Fraser Tytler (1791–1849), an Edinburgh law graduate and a
member of a distinguished legal and academic family, Tory in politics, was influenced by Walter Scott from childhood, and accepted his
proposal in 1823 to write a new history of Scotland.[11] This was to take
advantage of the recent ordering of the public records of Scotland by
the Bannatyne Club and the retrieval of a great amount of lost information. Although he was to insist on painstaking scrutiny and strict
evaluation of original sources, this was not always clear from his writings, where 'he abjured repetitive or tenuous citations'.

Between 1826 and 1843 he brought out eight volumes, covering
from Alexander III in 1249 to the Union of the Crowns in 1603.
Offended by criticism of deliberate bias – that they had been written
from an aristocratic, Tory, Episcopalian and unpatriotic point of view –
he finally moved to England. He had enjoyed demolishing old legends,
only to find that the Scots preferred comforting national myths.

Tytler covered the Battle of Harlaw in a chapter entitled 'Regency
of Albany', and it is necessary to reproduce this in detail, for this will
show that it was ever after copied, word for word, by historians who
followed, 'Highland' as well as 'Lowland', and including Walter Scott,
his mentor:

> He [Donald] contended that by Euphemia taking the veil, she
> became civilly dead; and that the earldom of Ross belonged
> lawfully to him, in right of Margaret his wife. His plea was at
> once repelled by the governor; and this noble territory, which
> included the Isle of Skye, and a district in the mainland equal in
> extent to a little kingdom, was declared to be the property of the
> Earl of Buchan. But the island prince, who had the pride and the
> power of an independent monarch, derided the award of Albany,
> and, collecting an army of ten thousand men, prepared not only
> to seize the disputed county, but determined to carry havoc and
> destruction into the heart of Scotland. Nor, in the midst of these
> ferocious designs, did he want [lack] somewhat of a statesman
> like policy; for he engaged in repeated alliances with England,
> and, as the naval force which he commanded was far superior
> to any Scottish fleet which could be brought against him, his
> cooperation with the English in their attacks upon the Scottish
> commerce, was likely to produce very serious effects.

Tytler did not know that Euphemia's entry to a nunnery was to be well after Harlaw, although he states the legal case correctly. Donald is portrayed as an 'island prince', determined on havoc and destruction, with the naval power to do so, and his backing of England through many earlier treaties of 1405 and 1408 – a Scottish magnate clearly beyond Crown control.

> When his preparations were completed, he at once broke in upon the earldom at the head of his fierce multitudes, who were armed after the fashion of their country, with swords fitted to both cut and thrust, pole-axes, bows and arrows, short knives and round bucklers formed of wood or strong hide, with bosses of brass or iron. The people of the county readily submitted to him – to have attempted opposition, indeed, was impossible – and these northern districts had for many centuries been more accustomed to pay their allegiance to Norwegian yarls, or pirate kings, whose power was at their door, than to acknowledge the remote superiority of the Scottish crown . . .
>
> The Lord of the Isles then ordered a general rendezvous of his army at Inverness, and sent his summons to levy all the fighting men in Boyne and Enzie, who were compelled to follow his banner and to join the soldiers from the Isles; with this united force, consisting of the flower of the island and northern chivalry, he swept through Moray, meeting with none, but the most feeble resistance; while his soldiers covered the land like locusts, and the plunder of money, arms and provisions daily gave them new strength, spirits and energy. Strathbolgy was next invaded, and the extensive district of Garryach, which belonged to his rival the Earl of Mar, was delivered up to cruel and indiscriminate havoc.
>
> It had been the boast of the Island Prince that he would burn the rich burgh of Aberdeen, and make a desert of the country to the shores of the Tay; and as the smoke of his camp-fires was already seen on the banks of the Don, the unhappy burghers began to tremble in their booths, and to anticipate the realization of these dreadful menaces.

Although he gives no other sources for his detailed and credible description, especially of the invader's arms, Tytler's single footnote indicates that he has simply elaborated greatly the account given by Bower, where Donald's gathering force – but now described as the flower of chivalry despite their locust-like plundering of the region – is set not only upon the destruction of Aberdeen, but also of the country down to the Tay.

> But their spirits soon rose when the Earl of Mar, whose reputation as a military leader was of the highest order, appeared at the head of an army, composed of the bravest knights and gentlemen in Angus and the Mearns; and declared his resolution of instantly advancing against the invader. Mar had the advantage of having been bred up in the midst of Highland war, and at first distinguished himself, as we have seen, at the head of the ketherans. But his marriage with the Countess of Mar, and his reception at court, appear to have effectively changed his character; the fierce and savage habits of his early life were softened down, and left behind them a talent for war, and an ambition for renown, which restlessly sought for employment whenever there was a chance of gaining distinction ... his reputation abroad was as distinguished as at home. In a very short time he found himself at the head of the whole power of Mar and Garryach, in addition to that of Angus and the Mearns; Sir Alexander Ogilvy, sheriff of Angus, Sir James Scrymgeour, constable of Dundee and hereditary standard-bearer of Scotland, Sir Alexander Irvine, Sir Robert Melville, Sir William de Abernethy, nephew to Albany, and many other barons and esquires, with their feudal services, joined him with displayed banner; and Sir Robert Davidson, the provost of Aberdeen, and a troop of the stoutest burgesses, came boldly forward to defend their hearths and their stalls from the ravages of the Island King.

Tytler appears to follow Bower, the only source for Mar's early disreputable career as leader of a band of wild Highlanders, and brushes over his dubious method of obtaining the Earldom to paint the picture of a reformed hero, battle hardened, a court favourite well capable of leading the attack against Donald.

> Mar immediately advanced from Aberdeen, and marching by Inverury came in sight of the Highlanders at the village of Harlaw, on the water of Ury, not far from its junction with the Don. He found that his little army was immensely outnumbered, it is said, by nearly ten to one; but it consisted of the bravest barons in

these parts; and his experience had taught him to consider a single knight in steel as a fair match against a whole troop of ketherans. Without delay, he entrusted the leading of the vaward [vanguard] to the constable of Dundee, and Ogilvy, the sheriff of Angus, who had with them a small but compact battalion of knights and men-at-arms; whilst he himself followed with the rearward, composed of the main strength of his army, including the Irvings of Drum, the Maules, the Morays, the Straitons, the Lesleys, the Stirlings, the Lovels, headed by their chiefs, and with their banners and penoncelles waving amid their grove of spears. Of the Islesmen and highlanders, the principal leaders were the lord of the isles himself, with Macintosh and Maclean, the heads of their respective septs, and innumerable other chiefs and chieftains, animated by the old and deep-rooted hostility between the Celtic and Saxon race.

Walter Scott, Tytler's mentor, quotes from the above for *his* description of the battle in his *Tales of a Grandfather*, published in the same year (1828), but Tytler gave no sources for his own version, the scene now romantically embellished with all flags flying, and with combatants taken from Abercromby and the *Don: A poem*:

The shock between two such armies may be easily imagined to have been awful; the highlanders, who were ten thousand strong, rushing on with the fierce shouts and yells which it was their custom to raise in coming in to battle, and the knights meeting them with levelled spears, and ponderous maces and battle-axes, which inflicted ghastly wounds upon their half-armed opponents. In his first onset, Scrymgeour, and the knights and bannerets who fought under him, with little difficulty drove back the mass of the Islesmen, and cutting his way through their thick columns, made a dreadful slaughter: But though hundreds fell around him, thousands poured in to supply their place, more fierce and fresh than their predecessors, whilst Mar, who had penetrated with his main army into the very heart of the enemy, found himself in the same difficulties, becoming every moment more tired with slaughter, more encumbered with the numbers of the slain, and less able to resist the increasing ferocity and reckless courage of the masses that stilled yelled and fought around him. It was impossible that this should continue much

longer without making a fatal impression against the Scots, and
the effects of fatigue were soon seen. The Constable of Dundee
was soon slain, and the highlanders, encouraged by his fall,
wielded their broadswords and Lochaber axes with murderous
effect, seizing and stabbing the horses, and pulling down their
riders, whom they despatched with their short daggers.

Tytler again gives no sources for all these gory details, perhaps com-
bining his imagination with the creative accounts of foot soldier Scots
bringing down English knights at Bannockburn (to which he refers
further on in his history):

In this way were slain some of the best and bravest soldiers of
these northern districts. Sir Robert Davidson, with the greater
part of the stalwart burgesses who fought around him, were
amongst the number; and many of the families lost not only their
chief, but every male in the house. Lesley of Balquhain, a baron
of noble and ancient lineage, is said to have fallen, with six of his
sons slain beside him. The sheriff of Angus, with his eldest son
George Ogilvy, Sir Alexander Irving of Drum, Sir Robert Maule,
Sir Thomas Moray, William Abernethy, Alexander Straiton
of Lauriston, James Lovel, Alexander Stirling, and above five
hundred men-at-arms, including the principal gentry of Buchan,
shared their fate, whilst Mar himself, and a small number of survi-
vors, still continued the battle till nightfall; when the slaughter
ceased, and it was found in the morning that the Island Lord
had retreated by Inverury and the hill of Benochie, checked and
broken certainly by the desperate contest, but neither conquered
nor very effectually repulsed. Mar, on the contrary, although he
passed the night on the field, did so, not in the triumphant asser-
tion of victory, but from the effects of wounds and exhaustion;
the best and the bravest of his friends were stretched in their
last sleep around him, and he found himself totally unable to
pursue the retreat of the Islesmen. Amongst those of the highlanders who fell were the chiefs of Maclean and Mackintosh,
with upwards of nine hundred men; a small loss compared with
that sustained by the lowlanders. The battle was fought on St.
James's Even, the twenty-fourth of July, and from the ferocity
with which it was contested, and the dismal spectacle of civil

war and bloodshed exhibited to the country, it appears to have
made a deep impression on the national mind.

Tytler adds how Albany collected an army in the autumn, marched
in person to Dingwall, made himself master of its castle, appointed
a governor, and repossessed Ross, while Donald fell back to his Isles.
Albany attacked the following summer and compelled Donald to give
up his independence and his claim to the Earldom of Ross, to become
a vassal and deliver hostages. This was followed by a six-year truce
with England.

Tytler notes the story that 'the Laird of Maclean was slain by Sir
Alexander Irvine', but otherwise the gist of his history conforms to
those given in the Latin chronicles, especially that there was no decisive victory after a ferocious conflict (although Boece stated that both
sides actually left the battlefield at nightfall). But the last places Donald
would have retreated through would have been through Mar's forces
(which Tytler leaves on the battlefield) and down from the plateau into
Inverurie, Mar's original muster point. Thereafter crossing the Ury
and going westwards via Bennachie would have taken Donald past
the belligerent Leslie's castle of Balquhain and straight into Forbes-
guarded territory.

On top of his giving no new evidence for his overall stirringly
romantic account, this aberration alone is worrying. How much
of Tyler's history came from his imagination, stirred by his mentor,
Walter Scott? It is concerning that those writers who followed, copied
Tytler, often word for word.

1838. *An Historical and Genealogical Account of the Clan MacLean from its First Settlement at Castle Duart, in the Isle of Mull, to the Present Period,* by a Seneachie[12]

Sir Alexander Irvine of Drum – 'outstanding for his great strength' –
was the only North-East noble described by the medieval chroniclers
as perishing at the Battle of Harlaw. His name was to become indis-
solubly linked by later historians to one of the greatest members of
Clan MacLean, 'Red Hector of the Battles':

Eachuinn Ruadhndn Cath (Hector Rufus Bellicosus ... distinguished himself in many daring exploits, and was esteemed one
of the most accomplished knights ... one of the best swordsmen

of his age ... His marriage to a daughter of the Earl of Douglas greatly enlarged his influence; and that nobleman made many overtures to induce Hector to withdraw himself from his dangerous connexion with his uncle Donald, Lord of the Isles and Earl of Ross, now on the brink of open war, if not with the government of the country, at least with him who then held the sovereign power, —Murdoch Duke of Albany, regent of the kingdom.

... the occasion promised too glorious a field for the genius of the warlike Lord of Duart to admit of his listening to any overture which would deprive him of a conspicuous share in the contest; besides, his being the hereditary lieutenant-general of the Isles gave his uncle a claim to his support ...

The whole array of the Isles, consisting of ten thousand warriors, was mustered for the approaching conflict; and Donald of the Isles (Earl of Ross), with the chief of Duart as his lieutenant, took the field at its head. The insular prince scoured the country eastward before him, and proceeded onwards, contemplating an attack by surprise upon Aberdeen, in which the head quarters of the regent's forces under the immediate command of the Earl of Marr then lay; but being anticipated by the enemy, who concentrated himself a few miles in advance of Aberdeen in Macdonald's route, the celebrated battle of Harlaw was fought, at the village of that name, about Whitsuntide in the year 1411.

In this battle the renowned chief of Maclean performed prodigies of valour; his massive sword, wielded by an arm already known for deeds of death, laid prostrate every foe it encountered; the battle raged amid the most dreadful havoc and carnage on both sides. In the after part of the day, while victory yet weighed the balance with an even hand for either side, the Lord of Duart met an adversary worthy his sanguinary claymore, Sir Alexander Irvine of Drum, of whose prowess he had often heard.

They were guided to one another by the armorial bearings on their shields.[6] 'Ha! chief of Duart, follower of a rebel vassal, have I at length the satisfaction to see thee within reach of my sword's point,' exclaimed the knight of Drum.— 'Time-serving slave,' replied Maclean, 'thou hast, if it be satisfaction to thee, and if my steel be as keen as my appetite for life of thine thou shalt not have time to repeat thy taunt.' The result was not of long duration, for such was the fury with which the heroic rivals fought that they fell dead foot to foot on the field, ere a friend had time to aid either. Thus fell 'Eachuinn Ruadh na 'n Cath,' in a way we may conclude the most congenial to such a spirit, 'With his back to the field, and his feet to the foe.' His remains were carried from the field of battle by the two subordinate clans of McInnes and McIlvurrich, and conveyed to Iona, where he was interred.

The anniversary of the battle of Harlaw was for many generations observed by the houses of Duart and Drum; and on such occasions an exchange of swords took place between the respective successors of Maclean and Irvine, as a token of respect to the memory of their brave ancestors, and as a bond of perpetual friendship between themselves.

It is a matter of doubt with all historians to the present day which side could claim a victory at Harlaw ; it appears decidedly to have been a drawn battle. Many valiant knights and gentlemen fell on both sides, and the loss in other respects appears to have been equal; the night alone separated the combatants, and neither party, as if afraid the one of the other, seemed disposed to renew hostilities. It is true, however, that the Lord of the Isles kept possession of the earldom of Ross, and maintained his right, which after his death was conceded to his son Alexander by King James I.

This death by mutual combat of Irvine of Drum and Hector Maclean is first mentioned by the Sleat historian in the late seventeenth century, but the above story that their families met thereafter on the anniversary of the battle to exchange swords does not appear in print until 1734.[13] As will be seen, in Lowland accounts it appears very much later, in Forbes Leslie's 1909 history, *The Irvines of Drum*.

It is curious that, as was seen in the *Books of Clanranald* in Chapter 5, the Gaels confused Murdoch with the real 'villain in the play', his father, Robert, Duke of Albany.

8

The Later Nineteenth-century Accounts

1845. 'Parish of the Chapel of Garioch', in *The New Statistical Account of Scotland*, by the Reverend Henry Simson[1]

That Tytler's history was to become extraordinarily influential can be seen in this account of the Battle of Harlaw, for the Reverend Henry Simson (1788–1850) copies Tytler word for word, footnotes included. He does, however, pick up on Tytler's 'topographical error', i.e. that Donald retreated via Inverurie and west past Bennachie, through the rear of Mar's army, and not back northwards 'through the gorges of the Foudland hills' along the route by which he had invaded.

This North-East Free Church minister, however, felt able to add several pages of considerable detail from his own investigations and local knowledge:

> In the immediate neighbourhood, two cairns were opened a few years ago . . . [Beaker folk cyst burials]. There are other two cairns upon the field of battle, still left untouched. The one, as formerly mentioned, is called Drum's Cairn and the other Maclean's Grave.*
>
> * In the year of 1837, when the tenant at Harlaw was trenching a piece of barren ground, about a quarter of a mile to the north of the field of battle, he dug up the bones of about twelve human bodies. Part of a scull, and of the thigh bones, are in the possession of the writer hereof...
>
> The field upon which, it is said, the battle was fought, is about a quarter of a mile south-east of the farm of Harlaw, and still goes by the name of the *Pley Fauld* [the disputed cattle pen]. About a hundred yards to the west of the said farm, is to be seen a large whinstone, about 7 feet in height and 2 in breadth, which is called the *Liggar's Stane*, [invaders' camp marker] and which is said to have been put in its present situation, to mark the spot

where the females who followed the soldiers, and who were slain in battle, were buried.

To the west of the field of battle about half a mile, is a farmer's house called *Legget's Den** [Legate's Den], hard by, in which is a tomb . . . where, as the country people generally report, Donald of the Isles lies buried, being slain in battle, and therefore they call it commonly Donald's Tomb. It is certain, however, says Tytler, that the Lord of the Isles was not slain. This may probably be the tomb of the chief of Maclean or Macintosh, both of whom fell in battle.

> * There is a tradition still prevalent in this parish, that this farm was so named in consequence of a conference having been held there, between one of the Kings of Scotland and a Pope's legate.

Douglas Simpson described this as, 'Perhaps the best exposition of what may be called the popular view of the battle.'[2] Yet to a slavish dependence upon Tytler (Donald was not killed and buried there, nor was Macintosh) the Reverend Henry Simson added the way in which local legend vividly embellished and 'explained' the battle. Female camp followers would have been an unlikely addition to Donald's fast-moving force. The fauld described by the 'Sleat historian' into which Mar's cowards escaped makes its appearance. In the 1970s, a local farmer recounted that Leggat's Den was so called because a papal legate had attempted to intervene and stop the battle.[3] This accords with the similar attempt made by the Bishop of Aberdeen, which was mentioned in the Irvine-Fortescue papers.[4]

1863. 'The Burghers of Bon-Accord', in *Ballads from Scottish History*, by Norval Clyne[5]

An Aberdeen advocate, born and bred in the city, educated at its Grammar School and Marischal College, Norval Clyne (1817–1888) was both poet and ballad authority, with a considerable knowledge of Aberdeen's earliest records, both civil and ecclesiastical.[6] It is therefore not surprising that most of his interest in the Battle of Harlaw was focused on Provost Davidson and his friendship with the Earl of Mar, together with the burgesses who accompanied him to Harlaw, as follows:

This battle was occasioned by the inroad of Donald, Lord of the Isles, upon the Northern Lowlands, arising from a dispute between that chief and Robert, Duke of Albany, Regent of Scotland, concerning the succession to the Earldom of Ross. The Islesmen, on coming to Harlaw, near Inverury, and about eighteen miles north-west of Aberdeen, were opposed by an army very much inferior to their own in numbers, commanded by Alexander Stewart, Earl of Mar, who had hastily gathered to his standard the barons and gentlemen of Aberdeenshire, Angus and the Mearns. The burgesses of Aberdeen (well known by its ancient motto of 'Bon-accord') were led out by Robert Davidson, the 'Alderman' or Provost for the time, and greatly distinguished themselves in the bloody engagement which ensued.

The result of the conflict saved not only the town of Aberdeen, but a great part of Scotland from the evils which the conquest of a civilised territory by the savage katerans would certainly have occasioned. The Lord of the Isles used no greater threat than he might easily have fulfilled, but for the determined resistance thus made to the design he expressed, of plundering Aberdeen, and over-running the country to the banks of the Tay. In the battle Provost Davidson was slain, along with a number of his fellow-citizens. His body was brought to Aberdeen, and interred within the parish church of St. Nicholas.

It is characteristic of an age when the sword was wielded more readily than the pen, to find in the contemporary municipal record no mention of the battle which had deprived the community of the chief magistrate whom they had chosen at the preceding Michaelmas. That record, however, contains a list of burgesses who were 'chosen to go out against the katerans' [*Electi ad transeundum contra Kethranos*]. It is found in the 1st volume of the Council Register (MS), p. 291 . . . and has the appearance of being hastily written out upon a page previously left blank, and originally intended for a more peaceful entry. There seems good reason for assigning it to a date corresponding to the conflict at Harlaw, and is too interesting to be omitted here.

Clyne then named the thirty-three burgesses, noting that there were five more whose names had been scored through. He considered Walter Scott's story that after the battle 'the town made an act that in the future their Provost should upon no occasion, whether of war or ceremony, go beyond the gates' to be 'scarcely credible' – although there is in fact a blank in the record from 1414 to 1433. Clyne then published in full the 'before 1600' Harlaw ballad published by Ramsay, discussed the pros and cons of it having been the ballad mentioned in the *Complaynt of Scotland*, and stated that he intended to prove that it was composed by someone who had Boece's Latin account before him.

To this end he reproduced Boece's Latin version in full (with a few transcription errors) and detailed how it corresponded both in fact and error with Boece's version (and not with his later translation by Bellenden) rather than with those given by Bower and Mair. He suggested as the author, 'A scholarly person, and an alumnus, perhaps, of the College at Aberdeen of which Boece was the first Principal; at all events a native of the north country, not unfamiliar with the district'.

1867. 'Regency of Albanys', in *The History of Scotland*, by John Hill Burton[7]

As with Norval Clyne, John Hill Burton (1809–1881)was an Aberdonian lawyer, educated at the Grammar School and Marischal College, who made his name as a journalist, political economist, and historian. He was appointed historiographer-royal of Scotland in 1867, and commenced the editing of *The Register of the Privy Council of Scotland* ten years later. His historical writings have been described as 'drily critical, not to say antiquarian' in character, and like Clyne, he was an Episcopalian, with Conservative and Jacobite sympathies.[8] He considered Harlaw to have been 'a great battle, arising out of dangers and difficulties of a new and special kind', which was 'the final struggle for supremacy between the Highland and the Lowlands'.

His introduction to the actual conflict described how the western Scots (descended from Irish colonisers) were 'ever shy and troublesome as subjects of the King of Scotland, and were sometimes entirely independent of his rule'. With the ending of Norse rule of the western seaboard, he maintained that 'the Celts predominated', albeit with 'a strong element of Norse blood'. They opposed Bruce and allied themselves with England during the War of Independence, and England's war with France. If the Teutonic and Celtic populations had ever been mixed, there arose a clear line of demarcation. 'The Goth' had now got far ahead of the Celt as a leader of civilisation: one farmed peacefully, the other lived idly and seized upon their neighbour's riches. The heiress of the Earldom of Ross 'retired from the world, and took the veil', but Donald's claim to the Earldom, through marriage to her aunt, which would have made him 'lord or monarch of about half of Scotland', was understandably refused as 'policy of the government'. Hill Burton continued:

> On the ground that he was treated with gross injustice, Donald resolved on war.
>
> In the summer of 1411, the agriculturists and burghers of the North were appalled by the rumour that a body of marauding Highlanders of unparalled force – on the scale, indeed, of a considerable army – was coming upon them to pillage and burn, and conquer Scotland to the Tay. The force was reputed to amount to ten thousand. That might not seem overwhelming to a country that had dealt with the great English invasions, but it was the districts exempt from these that was threatened, and the invasion was, in fact, an attack in the rear. It took the country by surprise, and there was a hasty gathering of the gentry, with their tenants, and the burgher force of the towns. They could muster a small body only, but it was a high spirited, efficient force, well armed. It was commanded by the Earl of Mar, whom we have lately found in different company. He had gained experience in the French wars, and several of his followers possessed the same advantage.
>
> Donald and his host came through the northern mountains to Benochie, near the Don in Aberdeenshire. This hill is the last bastion of the Grampians abutting into the Lowlands. From its top one can see, towards the west, mountain after mountain rolling away upwards to the highest of the Grampians; on the other side spreads to the coast a plain as flat as Lincolnshire. Donald kept on the shoulder of this outstretching hill till he descended to the flat country, as if reluctant to leave the rough mountain ground to which his followers were accustomed. At Harlaw, on the flat moor edging up the rise of the hill, he met those who had come to guard the entrance to the low country. The usual rush of the Highlanders was met by a compact body of men-at-arms and spearmen, who held their own firmly. The numbers of the Highlanders, however, enabled them, wasteful as they were of life, to dash, wave after wave as it were, against the

compact little body; and the chances were, that by giving several lives for each one, the Highlanders might annihilate their opponents. These held out, however, and Donald had to retreat; there was no great victory gained over him, but he was stopped in his career, and that was everything.

Hill Burton mistakenly situated Donald a mountain range too much to the south, on the shoulder of Bennachie, and then had to have him descending to 'the flat country', to get to the plateau of Harlaw, i.e. not only skirting the fortress of Balquhain, but crossing the flood plain of the Ury to get *up* to the battlefield. Now it was the Highlanders who attacked Mar's 'compact body' in wave after wave, only to produce a stalemate. There was no mention of any summer day's dreadful slogging match, ended only by exhaustion of both sides and by nightfall.

Hill Burton, moreover, does not leave the battle as merely putting a stop to marauding Highlanders, as had been achieved in the past. It was especially not just an episode in a 'civil war'. That would have been an irrational concept; it was a contest between foes who had never been 'in harmony with each other', or had ever had 'a feeling of common interests and common nationality'. As he saw it, however, although the enemy were *caterans*, they had been driven to this state of desperation by a 'long succession of penal and denunciatory laws against the Highlanders', from a 1384 Act onwards, laws increasingly cruel in their effect. To him, Harlaw was one of Scotland's most memorable battles.

> It will be difficult to make those not familiar with the tone and feeling in Lowland at that time believe that the defeat of Donald of the Isles was felt as a more memorable deliverance even than that of Bannockburn. What it was to be subject to England the country knew and disliked; to be subdued by their savage enemies of the mountains opened to them sources of terror of unknown character and extent.

1878. 'The Battle of Harlaw and its Times', in *Inverurie and the Earldom of the Garioch*, by John Davidson[9]

The Reverend John Davidson (1816–1892), born and bred in Aberdeen and educated at Marischal College (honours MA in 1838; Doctorate of Divinity in 1877), served as minister to Inverurie from 1844 until his death, and published the above anthology of historical notes and genealogies concerning the people of the Garioch.[10]

He gives the most detailed account of the Battle of Harlaw, seven thousand words long – and the one on which modern versions are mainly based. Yet the warning given by Aberdeen University's Librarian, Douglas Simpson, an authority on the history of the region, especially its castles, should be noted; he considered this account was an 'imaginative reconstruction', in places 'pure flight of fancy, unsupported by any evidence'.

Although Davidson also leant heavily on Tytler (again sometimes word for word) for his histories, he displayed a remarkable grasp of the genealogies of the region's families in order to show their involvement in the battle. Or rather, what he considered *must* have been their involvement, for his accounts were prefaced quite honestly with 'they would', 'we can name [suggest]', 'one would willingly imagine', 'would doubtless', 'would proceed', 'would find', 'would see', and suchlike qualifications. His basic assumption throughout was that if families lived in the Garioch and the North-East region, 'it is likely' they fought at Harlaw, although he could only name Irvine of Drum, the only 'local' noble present at the battle, as the Latin chroniclers had also said.

Nevertheless, he very imaginatively described no fewer than three attacking columns, with Mar leading the centre, and had them converge on Donald's forces at Harlaw. From his sound local knowledge he described the lie of the land: on the west, the steep slope down to the soft bed of the Ury; on the east a wide morass of the Lochter Burn; in the centre, up the braes of Balhaggardy, a 'narrow platform' for attack, unsuitable for cavalry, 'more adapted to the crowded wrestle which the Highlanders made the battle become'.

An Inverurie minister could well see that on such ground there would have been no glorious charge of knightly horsemen in glittering array, battle pennons flying, yet he then goes on to quote Tytler's fanciful descriptions. Donald's army was again listed as ten thousand strong, with Mar's 'only about a tenth of that amount', although advantageously composed of 'fully equipped knights and men-at-arms'. John Davidson had Mar placing the Constable of Dundee and the Sheriff of Angus at the front, along with, 'it is likely', Provost Davidson and his burgesses. Mar brings up the main army in the centre, with his Angus and Mearns people; there are Irvines, Leiths, Leslies and Gordons on the left, and Keiths and Forbeses, 'it would seem', on the right.

He mentioned the Irvine/Maclean fatal combat together with 'another romantic legend' which stated that Irvine of Drum, on the way to the battle, had a presentiment of death, and sat down with his brother on a large 'yird stane' [the Drum Stone] to make a 'tesment' that should he die, his brother was to marry his virgin widow (whom he claimed he had married unwillingly and never slept with), for then 'his lands would be his'. Davidson doubted this story, as Irvine had a legitimate son Alexander, who appears in post-Harlaw charters. He thus discounted the legend that these charters refer to Irvine's brother conveniently adopting the name 'Alexander' and inheriting both title and lands.

Other than Tytler, his written sources are given as *Don: A poem*, and both the 'Ramsay ballad' and the 'Forbes ballad' – this last reproduced almost entirely. From where had the minister of Inverurie, John Davidson, gained what would appear to be the complete details of the battle, the combatants, the modes of fighting, and the names and families of those who fought? Details which far surpassed those given by earlier sources, even Abercromby? Did such fine detail survive in oral memories and local traditions after more than four hundred and fifty years? Even the family histories of the Forbes and Irvine-Fortescues do not provide such a level of information, and the late James Irvine-Fortescue of Kingcausie himself wrote: 'I have not found any account of Harlaw or any detail of the Irvine/McLean contest among the Drum papers.'[12] Did Davidson have access to documents no longer in existence? Or was he assuming that the North-East families, whose histories he had researched so well, *must* have been present, despite their absence from the Latin accounts?

1881. 'Donald, Second Lord of the Isles', in *History of the MacDonalds*, by Alexander Mackenzie[13]

Alexander Mackenzie (1838–1898), an Inverness historian and author of numerous clan histories, became an editor and publisher of the *Celtic Magazine* and the *Scottish Highlander*. In 1894, the Gaelic Society of Inverness elected him as an 'Honorary Chieftain'. He gives the following account:

> He [Donald] was a man of distinguished ability, and, although so closely connected with the throne, he resolved to gain complete independence, like his ancestors, for the Island kingdom. The

more easily to gain his purpose he entered into an alliance with
the English against his own country and king, a proceeding which
can only be justified on the plea that, like his predecessors, he
considered himself an independent Prince, owing no allegiance
to the Scottish king for the territories held by the race of Somerled
in the north-west Highlands and Isles. This contention was,
however, clearly untenable, for in point of fact he only possessed
his lands, as the eldest son of the *second* marriage, by a charter
from the crown . . . Be that as it may, it is undisputed that the
second Lord of the Isles is found, in the year 1388, shortly after
the death of his father, negotiating with Richard II of England on
the footing of an independent Prince . . .

A few years later Donald raised the flag of rebellion, and con-
ducted himself in a manner, and exhibited a power and capacity,
which shook the throne and government to their very foundations.

Thus Mackenzie claimed that Donald sought complete independence
from the Scottish Crown, and pursued this via a disturbing alliance
with England, behaving as an 'independent Prince' in his dealings both
with Richard II (and later with Henry IV in 1400, 1405 and 1408):

He had married Lady Mary Leslie, only daughter of the Countess
of Ross. Alexander, Earl of Ross, her only brother, married Isabella
Stewart, daughter of the Regent, Robert Duke of Albany, by which
union he had an only child, Euphemia, who became a nun, and
resigned her estates and dignities in favour of her grandfather
and her uncle, John, Earl of Buchan, second son of the Duke of
Albany, and his heirs male, whom failing, to return to the Crown,
thus cutting off Lady Margaret, the wife of Donald, who was the
heir general . . . Donald saw it that if Albany was permitted to
retain actual possession of the Earldom, he would be unable to
recover it in right of his wife from that crafty nobleman.

He accordingly proceeded to take possession, contending that
Euphemia, by taking the veil, had become in a legal point of view,
dead; and that the Earldom belonged to him in right of his wife.
His demand that he should on these grounds be put in possession of it was opposed by the Governor, whose principal object
appears to have been to prevent the accession of so vast a district
as the ancient Earldom of Ross to the extensive territories of the

Lord of the Isles, already too powerful to be kept in check by the Government. The Governor was actuated more by what would most conduce to the security of the Government than by any question as to whether the claims of the Lord of the Isles were in themselves just or not.

... no sooner did he receive an unfavourable denial of this demands than he collected all the forces he could command, amounting to about ten thousand men, with whom he invaded the Earldom. He appears to have met no resistance from the people of Ross; and soon obtained possession of that district.

Despite demonstrating that Donald had a strong legal argument, and despite Albany's machinations (although Euphemia was not to resign her rights until 1415), Mackenzie maintained 'that crafty noblemen', as Governor of Scotland, was quite right to deny Donald the vast Earldom of Ross, for this would have turned him into a veritable prince and a danger to the stability of the Government – as indeed his violent actions were soon to show.

Donald Gregory's *History of the Western Highlands and Islands of Scotland* has been described as 'the *fons et origo* of modern scholarly historical writing on the late medieval Gàidhealtachd.' [14] He also felt that Albany would have rightly been suspicious of Donald's dealings with England.[15]

Surprisingly, Mackenzie then proceeded to quote from the 1837 *The Highlanders of Scotland.*[16] It had been written by William Skene, the son of a close friend of Walter Scott's – and it showed:

Donald was now in complete possession of the earldom, but his subsequent proceedings showed that the nominal object of his expedition was but a cover to ulterior designs; for, leaving the district of Ross, he swept through Moray and penetrated into Aberdeenshire, at the head of his whole army. Here he was met at the village of Harlaw by the Earl of Mar, at the head of an inferior army in point of numbers, but composed of Lowland gentlemen who were better armed and better disciplined than the Highland followers of Donald. It was on the 24th July, 1411, that the celebrated battle of Harlaw was fought, upon the issue of which seemed to depend the question of whether the Gaelic or Teutonic part of Scotland were in future to have the supremacy. [17]

Mackenzie followed this with a detailed description of the battle, again lifted almost word for word from Tytler, but with additional Romantic flourishes such as, 'surrounded on all sides, no alternative remained for Sir James and his valorous companions but victory or death, and the latter was their lot'. Tytler had merely claimed the remarkably ferocious battle was 'a dismal spectacle of civil war and bloodshed', but for Mackenzie, 'It was the final contest for supremacy between Celt and Teuton'. This racial dualism appeared 'to have made at the time an inconceivably deep impression on the national mind'.

To finish up, he repeats the version of the battle given by the 'Sleat historian', but then surprisingly repeats Hill Burton's firm opinion that the battle was not only a defeat for Donald, but also 'a more memorable deliverance [from the wild Highlanders] than even that of Bannockburn'.

The influence of Scott and Tytler followers was long-lasting, but two remarkable ministers, historians of Clan Donald, were to sweep it aside.

1896. 'Donald of Harlaw', in *The Clan Donald,* by Reverend Angus MacDonald and Reverend Archibald MacDonald

Written by Angus MacDonald (1860–1932), minister of Killearnan, a historian and anthologist, together with his neighbour Archibald MacDonald (1853–1946), minister of Kiltarlity, a historian and genealogist, this encyclopaedic history of the Clan Donald in three volumes contains in Chapter VII of the first volume the lead-up to the battle, the battle itself, and its aftermath.[18]

Donald's valid but disputed claim to the Earldom of Ross is ascribed variously to the rumours that Euphemia had resigned her rights, or that she was 'sickly, some say, deformed, and not likely to live long' and 'to have a call from heaven'. The authors begin by affirming that: 'Unquestionably the occasion of unfurling the Macdonald banner at this time was the conduct of Albany, in relation to the disputed succession to the Earldom of Ross'. Donald, furthermore, 'had no higher ambition than to make himself master of that extensive territory', and 'In addition to the conquest of Ross, it is said that Donald had other designs, but it is difficult to conceive what these could have been. The wild and extensive scheme which historians have alleged Donald to have conceived of making himself master of all Scotland is too utterly incredible, and may be dismissed at once as unworthy of any consideration. The conflict, moreover, was not one between Celt and Saxon as such, nor was the struggle one for supremacy of the one race over the other.'

But circumstances were to change. The extent of the lands that the Earldom encompasses are detailed:

> The old district of Ross, Cromarty, and that portion of ancient Argyll extending westwards from Glenelg to Lochbroom, including the coast lands of Kintail, Lochalsh, Lochcarron, Applecross, and Gairloch. It extended inland as far east as Urquhart, and included the parish of Kilmorack . . .
>
> In addition to the foregoing the Earls of Ross were superiors of lands of which the following are the more important:- In the County of Aberdeen the lands of Auchterless and King Edward; in the county of Inverness, the lands of Innnermerky in the lordship of Badenoch; in the county of Nairn, the lands of Blamakayth, Both, Banchre, Rate, Kynowdie, Kinsteary, Kinravock, Easter Geddes, Drumnaglass, and Cawdor . . .
>
> The heather was soon aflame, and the fiery cross blazed through the Isles as well as those mainland regions in which the Macdonald power was predominant. The whole clan, with its vassals, rallied to the fight. From many a glen and strath, and isle, the Gaelic warriors hastened to the rendezvous, wherever the ancient banner of the Kings of Innsegall was unfurled to its native breeze. The Macleans and Mackinnons, the hardy clans of Mull, the Clan Chattan from lone Lochaber, the Macleods from the rugged hills of Harris and Lewis, obeyed the call to arms [to Ardtornish].

Disembarking his fleet at Strome, Donald marched his army towards Dingwall, encountering and defeating on the way to Inverness the fierce opposition of the 'Norse Celts' such as Clan Mackay from Caithness, and later the Mackenzies and Frasers. Circumstances had now changed and 'having Ross in his hands, was not enough for Donald'. He resolved to push his way eastwards, recruiting more men, 'presenting such a formidable and imposing appearance as to strike terror into the heart of the opposing host', and threatening to burn the town of Aberdeen.

The ministers dismissed 'the wild and extensive scheme which historians have alleged Donald to have conceived of making himself master of all Scotland' as 'too utterly incredible', and 'unworthy of any consideration'. As for any more ambitious plan of campaign in which Donald expected to join up with his English allies, they could only speculate that 'England's own difficulties in France proved Scotland's friends in need'; 'if Donald cherished any expectations of southern aid, he was doomed to disappointment'. The conflict, moreover, was not one between Celt and Saxon as such, nor was the struggle one for supremacy of the one race over the other.

They then assure us that any statements that Donald's army indiscriminately ravaged the countryside of Moray and Aberdeen, should 'be taken with a very large grain of salt', as parts were selectively put to fire and sword only if they refused to provide him with recruits, and not just to provide plunder for maintenance. The composition of his army of ten thousand differs little from that given by the 'Sleat historian', and concentrates on the principals – Maclean commanding the right wing, The Mackintosh the left, John Mor Tainister the reserve, with the chiefs of the Macleods of Lewis and Harris under Donald in the main body. The principals of Mar's force are 'the gentlemen of Aberdeen, Angus and the Mearns' as given by Abercromby. The *brosnachadh* incitement is supposedly sung, and the battle is engaged – again as per Tytler, but with anachronistic embellishments of 'plaided and kilted warriors who fought with claymore' against 'mail-clad mounted knights, armed to the teeth after the manner of Norman chivalry':

> The Highlanders, armed with broadswords, bows and axes, and wooden shields, rushing forward with furious onset and shouting the slogan of their clan, were received by the Lowlanders with steadiness and valour ... the contest raged with fury ... until the Lowland army was reduced to a skeleton ... The Lowland army was annihilated, and the flower of the chivalry of Angus and the Mearns lay dead upon the field ... To the East of Scotland, Harlaw was a miniature Flodden.

The mutual combat between Maclean and Irvine is mentioned but the list of the principal Lowland dead is again only that given in the Latin chronicles. Once again, with the exception of Irvine of Drum and Leslie of Balquhain, none of the many North-East families claimed to have been present by Abercromby and later historians would appear to have suffered any losses. As for the lies spread by Lowland chroniclers:

That Macdonald of the Isles at the head of 8000 [remaining] clansmen, or even half that number, retreated in dismay before a wounded leader [Mar] lying prostate on the field of battle surrounded by a mere handful of men, most of whom were crippled with wounds, cannot easily be believed by any unprejudiced person. If Donald ever expected English help, he now realised that he must do without it, and knowing well that all Lowland Scotland was arrayed against him, he judged it the wisest policy to betake himself to his Island fastnesses . . .

The Scottish historians, ignoring all such considerations, and blinded by race prejudices, have inferred from the retreat that followed what they call a drawn battle the defeat of Macdonald at Harlaw . . . the battle of Harlaw . . . resulted, as we have seen, in well nigh the total annihilation of the Lowland army.

This monumental, if sometimes imaginative history of Clan Donald makes three important 'Highland' claims about the battle: in no way was it the 'draw' claimed by the Lowland historians; Mar's army was 'annihilated'; as a result Donald withdrew wisely, well aware of the feuds and vengeance he was going to suffer from the rest of Scotland. They were adamant, moreover, that the conflict had not been between Celt and Saxon, nor a struggle for supremacy of the one race over the other.

Yet the ministers also gave their views of the Battle of Harlaw with a remarkable honesty: 'Trustworthy accounts of this famous fight there are none. Lowland historian and ballad composer, as well as Highland seanachie, described what they believed must and should have happened.'

9

Harlaw Legends and Myths

Concerning Sir Alexander Irvine of Drum

Not only was Sir Alexander Irvine of Drum the most fêted of the North-East nobles who took part in the Battle of Harlaw, but, as already noted, a number of personal histories have also been attached to him. These were that:

1. Irvine and Hector Maclean died in mutual combat.
2. The families of both men exchanged swords on the anniversary of the battle.
3. Irvine stopped on the way to the battle at the 'Drum Stone' to make his will.
4. Irvine requested, should he be killed, that his brother should marry his 'virgin' widow.

The mutual combat is attested early on by 'Sleat historian' in the late 1600s: 'On Macdonald's side Maclean fell; he and Irvin of Drum fought together until one killed the other.'

Abercromby in 1715 made no mention of it.

The Irvine-Fortescue papers in the 1720s not only detail the combat – set up between two champions in heroic style by the Bishop of Aberdeen – but also mention how one of Maclean's Highlanders cheated by knifing Irvine:

Laird of Drum was made choyce of as champion for the King and the Laird of Mcclene for the rebels . . . the two combatants formerly named wer no sooner engaged than both of them made it appear that ther pairties hade made a good choyse for they demonstrat so much courage, agility and strenth of body & limbs that it was hard for any Indefferent person (If there had been any ther) to make any conclusion upon the event till after a long and blody conflict both parties being rather wekened by loss of blood then any signs of relenting appearing it was Mcclens misfortoun to fall by Drums victorious hand and no less Drums misfortoun that one of the highland gentlemen who uas apoynted by the Rebell to be judge of Mcclens getting fair play cam first up to Drum and stabed him to the heart with a durk.

In Clan Maclean histories written in the 1730s this treachery has either been forgotten or discounted, for the families of both heroes are described as exchanging swords thereafter on the anniversary of the battle:

[Maclean] and Irvin of Drum seeking out one another by the Armorial Bearings on their shields met and killed one another . . . After the Battle of Harlaw there was a mutual Agreement 'twixt the Lairds of Drum and MacLean to exchange swords, which was kept up for a long Time by both Familys to cancel all Enmity for the future that might happen on Account of the above narrated Slaughter. Such another Agreement there was 'twixt the Families of Grant and Maclean.

(The description of this formal exchange as also being between the Macleans and the Grants is interesting. Was it a usual practice, a 'noble' way of preventing blood feuds, 'to cancel Enmity for the future'?)

The later Maclean historian 'Seanachie' in 1838 also insisted it was a fair fight, recounted now in early Victorian Romantic style:

They were guided to one another by the armorial bearings on their shields. 'Ha! chief of Duart, follower of a rebel vassal, have I at length the satisfaction to see thee within reach of my sword's point,' exclaimed the knight of Drum.— 'Time-serving slave,' replied Maclean, 'thou hast, if it be satisfaction to thee, and if my steel be as keen as my appetite for life of thine thou shalt not have time to repeat thy taunt.' The result was not of long duration, for such was the fury with which the heroic rivals fought that they fell dead foot to foot on the field, ere a friend had time to aid either.

A footnote made to the 1805 printing of *Don: A poem*, possibly by Charles Dawson, does mention 'a great stone, called Drum's Stone, in sight of Drum and Harlaw, upon which Drum made his testament.'

As noted in the last chapter, John Davidson in 1878 described 'another romantic legend', relating both the Irvine/Maclean fatal combat and the above story that Irvine of Drum, on the way to the battle, had a presentiment of death. He sat down with his brother on a large 'yird stane' [the Drum Stone] to make a 'tesment' that should he die, his brother was to marry his virgin widow (whom he claimed he had married unwillingly and never slept with), for then 'his lands would be his'. Davidson pointed out that Irvine had a legitimate son Alexander, who appears in post-Harlaw charters, and thus discounts the legend that these charters refer to Irvine's brother conveniently adopting the name 'Alexander' to inherit both title and lands.

1893. A Short Account of the Family of Drum in the County of Aberdeen, by Douglas Wimberley[1]

This author also mentions Irvine's mutually fatal single combat with Maclean, but follows John Davidson in discounting the story that Irvine, on the way to Harlaw, sat down on what was later to be known as the 'Drum Stone' on the hill of Auchronie and persuaded his brother Robert, who had accompanied him, to marry Elizabeth should he be killed (he describes the feud with the Keiths that the marriage of Elizabeth Keith to Alexander Irvine of Drum was intended to end). He also maintained that Alexander Irvine's son Alexander ('*secundus*') succeeded him, and that the son's marriage contract in the October following the battle neither states that he was marrying a 'virgin bride' of a deceased brother, nor that he had changed his name from Robert (or John). In fact both he and his brother Robert are both recorded afterwards as flourishing.

1909. The Irvines of Drum, by Jonathan Forbes Leslie[2]

This historian gives a well-annotated account of the lead-up to the battle but thereafter once more quotes Tytler, the 'Ramsay ballad' and Mair. He agrees with John Davidson and Wimberley in discounting the 'brother to marry the virgin bride' story, also maintaining that 'Harlaw' Alexander Irvine had a surviving son Alexander, ancestor of the Irvine of Drum's family line.[3] James Irvine-Fortescue had originally discounted the reference to this surviving son; he had maintained that the monumental brass in St Nicholas Kirk, Aberdeen, commemorating the Sir Alexander Irvine, who died in 1457, which describes him as '*secundus*' to his father, the 'Harlaw' Alexander, was not contemporary.[4] But the English Monumental Brass Society later affirmed that it was contemporary and was made in the Low Countries.[5]

Forbes Leslie records not only the Irvine/Maclean combat but also refers to the tradition of the sword exchange 'as a proof that no feud or animosity existed between the families'. The Irvines of Drum historian, Donald Mackintosh, claimed this was also in Maclean tradition.[6]

It would seem, therefore, that the story of the fight to the death between Irvine and Maclean is only first mentioned in a seventeenth-century account, and the exchange of swords does not appear until the eighteenth. Irvine's making of his will at the Drum Stone is not recorded until the start of the nineteenth century, and his brother being requested there to marry the 'virgin wife', and so doing after Irvine's death, does not make an appearance until the very end of that century.

A Battle between CELT and SAXON?

The historical perspectives through which the Battle of Harlaw has been viewed changed markedly from those of the early historians to those seen some three hundred years later. Attempting to find and pull any 'Celt v Saxon' thread from them all, however, does not mean ignoring the complex and ever-changing history of such important matters as the date of establishment of any 'Highland'/'Lowland' division, or the development of a 'Great Ill-Will of the Lowlander' supposedly held between peaceful, agricultural peoples and aggressive pastoral neighbours from the earliest times to the present day.[7]

Yet in describing the battle, chroniclers and historians have also revealed their views, opinions and prejudices concerning the combatants, as returning again to their histories will show.

The Early Histories

As will be recalled, the opinions of the mediaeval chroniclers were both succinct and in agreement, portraying Donald 'of the Isles' as an extremely powerful Scottish noble who had invaded mainland Scotland in an aggressive bid for the Earldom of Ross. Overcoming easily any initial resistance that he met from mainland Gaels in Ross, he had embarked further on a destructive *chevauchée* through the North and North-East of Scotland, with the intention of sacking Aberdeen. He was finally halted by Government forces led by the Earl of Mar, forces composed of nobles from the Spey to the Tay, at the indecisive but atrociously bloody Battle of Harlaw, from which he thereafter withdrew to his Isles.

These Latin chroniclers described the two opposing forces quite simply. Donald 'of the Isles' led 'Hebrideans' against 'the nobles' of the lands he was invading, whom they called the 'Scots on the opposing side', the forces of 'the government', or the 'southerners'. If the 'Ramsay ballad' can be taken as evidence, it describes the event as 'intestinal (civil) cruel strife'. Thus far there was no mention of any racial descriptions of either attackers or defenders, although it must be said that in his 1521 account Mair introduced the idea (although he did say this was only held by the 'common people') of 'wild Scots' fighting against 'civilised Scots'.

Although 'Wild Scots' is the usual translation for *sylvestres Scoti*, this might be better expressed as 'forest-dwelling Scots'. Authors from Virgil onwards had also used *silvester* to mean 'pastoral'. This alluded to the concept of a geographical subdivision of Scotland's peoples – those who inhabited sparse mountain regions and those who lived in the cultivatable lands. The two groups would thus naturally tend to differ both physically and mentally, one surviving by a more warlike, pastoral life as opposed to the more peaceable farming communities, a concept of 'barbarism versus civilisation' which goes back to the Romans and even earlier.

Yet it could be argued that such forests, (and indeed mountains) were actually much more typical of the lands inhabited by those opposing Donald, especially the inhabitants of the Earl of Mar's domains. Although such a geographical subdivision appears to have been the genesis of a much later Romantic concept of the 'hielands v. lawlans', the scene set so succinctly by the mediaeval writers, had simply been an invasion of the mainland by 'Islesmen/Hebrideans'. Only the 'Ramsay ballad' had described a slaughter 'of *Lowland* and of *Highland* men'.

Seventeenth-century Accounts

It will be recalled that, angered by accounts of Lowland chroniclers – especially Buchanan and Boece – the first known 'Highland' account of the Battle of Harlaw was written by the seventeenth-century Macdonald 'Sleat historian'.

The very important points that he wanted to make were, 'it is well known that the Islanders are as loyal and less injurious to their neighbours than any people in Scotland', and that after the battle Donald would not be 'tainted' or tempted 'to forsake the king [James] his cousin', despite the fact that during the king's captivity in England 'the Duke of Albany, the Regent, used all his power to oppose him [Donald] and impair his greatness, being vexed he that he had lost the battle of Harlaw'.

He described Donald's men as being both 'Islanders' (but ever loyal to the Crown) and also, at the actual battle, as 'his Highlanders' fighting against 'the Duke and his army'. 'Highlanders' presumably referred to those troops raised from Donald's mainland possessions, such as Glengarry, but this seems to be the beginning of the use of this term on its own to describe all his soldiers.

Eighteenth-century Accounts

The postscript in Scots to the *Brosnachadh* refers to those slain in Mar's army only as 'Low country people'.

Abercromby, in his 1771 *Martial Atchievements*, described how 'Donald of the Isles' (combined with Henry IV of England) was opposed by the 'Governor's forces', 'the Earl of Mar's party' of nobles 'from 'the Tay to the Spey'. On the other hand, Mar's Government army was simply seen as putting down 'domestic rebels'. Irvine-Fortescue had also downgraded 'Donald of the Isles' and his men to 'domestic rebels', against 'the King's commissioned Nobility, gentry & commons'. The heroic combat he described between Maclean and Irvine, arranged by the Bishop of Aberdeen, was relegated to a fight between a 'Rebell' and one of 'the King's partie'. Neither Celt nor Saxon has made an appearance.

Early Nineteenth-century Accounts

It is not until the start of the nineteenth century that Victorian historians of Harlaw, from either side, begin to introduce 'old and deep-rooted' racial reasons for Donald's foray, namely a 'hostility between Celtic and Saxon race'. This was but one aspect of how they re-created and vividly imagined the battle.

Walter Scott's first re-creation came with his famous 1816 *Antiquary* verses celebrating a clash between 'hieland and lawland', in which mail-clad horsemen of 'gentle Norman blude' easily rode down 'Highland kerne' clad inadequately in 'tartan plaids'. By the time he published *Ivanhoe* in 1819, however, he had changed his mind regarding brutal Normans sorely oppressing the noble Anglo-Saxons whom he was to celebrate thereafter as the saviours of Scotland. Yet in the same year Alexander Laing depicted the Harlaw forces only as 'an army composed of chiefs of the clans' versus 'the royalists' supporting 'the Stuarts'.

Scott returned to a grander scenario in his 1828 *Tales of a Grandfather*. At Harlaw, a 'Prince' in his own kingdom, called 'Donald of the Isles' met an 'inferior' army composed of 'brave gentlemen', 'Lowland gentlemen, better armed and disciplined'. This was now a desperate battle between 'Lowlanders' and 'Highlanders', for the latter were 'a wild and barbarous people' capable of overrunning a great part of 'the civilised country'. Fortunately, the 'barbarians' were halted, although at a great cost of lives on either side.

The following year Tytler painted a very similar picture of an 'island prince', 'Donald of the Isles', with the 'pride and power of an independent monarch', allied to England, who invaded at 'the head of a fierce multitude', 'the flower of the island and northern chivalry'; they first had to overcome the Gaels of the northern districts, who had been centuries too long under the influence of 'the Norwegian yarls'. Intent on locust-like destruction, especially of Aberdeen, the 'Highlanders' were halted at Harlaw by the Earl of Mar's outnumbered army 'composed of the bravest knights and gentlemen in Angus and the Mearns', the 'bravest barons', and 'stalwart burgesses'. Mar's previous experience as a 'head of the ketherens', 'in the midst of Highland war', was to stand him in good stead against Donald's 'Islesmen and highlanders' led by innumerable 'chiefs and chieftains'. But everyone, somehow, was 'animated by the old and deep-rooted hostility between the Celtic and Saxon race'.

It cannot have been easy, moreover, for Tytler to depict the combatants in a North-East invasion and battle as polarised in this poisonous way, even in his attempt to claim Harlaw as a place where the 'Highland' barbarians had once been successfully halted. A Scottish army had within living memory invaded England so deeply as to provoke an evacuation of London, but that had not been simply a matter of loyal 'Highlanders' fighting 'Lowlanders'. At the North-East Battle of Inverurie, for example, 'Highlanders' had indeed fought 'Lowlanders', but it was actually between the Highland Independent Companies, led by Norman MacLeod of MacLeod, on the Government side, and Lord Lewis Gordon defending Aberdeenshire for the Jacobites.

In his *Highlanders of Scotland* of 1837, William Forbes Skene described how at Harlaw, Donald's 'Highlanders' were opposed to Mar's 'Lowland gentlemen, who were better armed and disciplined than the Highland followers of Donald'. Skene concluded that the battle was fought 'on the issue of which seemed to depend the question of whether the Gaelic or Teutonic part of the population of Scotland were in future to have the supremacy'.

Over in Mull, a Clan Maclean historian in 1838 did not agree; he simply depicted Donald as leading 'the whole array of the Isles' and concentrated on the Romantic conflict between Irvine of Drum and Hector Maclean, with the families chivalrously exchanging swords thereafter on the anniversary of the battle. Any 'hostility' depicted between the 'heroic rivals' was displayed in the preliminary insults hurled between a 'time-serving slave', and a 'follower of a rebel vassal'. Another clan historian even claimed that the fight was the result of an 'ancient quarrel' between their families. This all had the atmosphere of an 'ordinary' battle for land and power in which 'many valiant knights and gentlemen fell on both sides'.

But from his parish in the Chapel of Garioch, in 1845 the Reverend Henry Simson had simply parroted Tytler when describing Harlaw, especially his 'old and deep-rooted hostility between the Celtic and Saxon races', adding that Provost Davidson and his burgesses 'came boldly forward to defend their hearths and stalls from the ravages of the Island King'.

Later Nineteenth-century Accounts

Racial hatred continue to resurge in Norval Clyne's 1863 account. Donald, 'Lord of the Isles', makes an inroad upon the 'Northern Lowlands', this time with 'Islesmen', only to be prevented by Mar and his hastily gathered 'burgesses, barons and gentlemen' of the region from making a 'conquest of a civilised territory by the savage katerans', as far down as 'the banks of the Tay'.

As far as Hill Burton was concerned in 1867, Harlaw was 'a great battle, arising out of dangers and difficulties of a new and special kind', i.e. the 'final struggle for supremacy between the Highlands and Lowlands'. With the ending of Norse rule of the western seaboard, 'the Celts predominated' although still with 'a strong element of Norse blood'. These Celts had allied themselves to England during the Wars of Independence, and a clear line of demarcation arose between the 'Teutonic and Celtic' populations, the former now leaders of civilisation and peaceful farming, the latter living idly by seizing their neighbours' riches.

His view was that Donald had invaded with a 'body of marauding Highlanders of unparalled force', intending to conquer Scotland down to the Tay, and had been blocked by a 'hasty gathering of the gentry, with their tenants, and the burgher force of the towns', who were terrified of being subdued by, and subject to 'their savage enemies of the mountains'.

Yet when the knowledgeable Aberdeenshire minister John Davidson described 'The Battle of Harlaw and its Times' in 1878, giving the longest and most detailed account to the battle, he made no mention of any dangers 'of a new and special kind'. On one side he had the 'rebels', i.e. 'Islesmen and their forced levies from Ross and Moray' (who are thereafter called 'Highlanders' at the battle itself) led by 'Donald of the Isles'. On the other, 'mailed Lowlanders' of the 'Regent's forces' led by the Earl of Mar, 'leader of the royalists', had no difficulty in piercing 'the masses of the Celts'.

Davidson felt that Harlaw had 'left a deep impression on the national mind', but although he relied heavily on Tytler, he did not support any racial view of the battle or the picture of barbarian 'Highlanders' challenging civilised 'Lowlanders' for the control of the country that Scott, Clyne and Hill Burton had described. It might seen that such scare-stories had died away as the century came to an end, but within a couple of years another Tytler adherent appeared from Inverness.

Alexander Mackenzie, in his 1881 *History of the MacDonalds*, simply quoted verbatim first Skene and then Tytler, with their 'Celt v. Teuton' views. He then switched back to the 'Sleat historian', with his descriptions of 'Highlanders' and 'Islanders' meeting Mar's 'Government army'.

The authors of the monumental 1896 *The Clan Donald*, the Reverend Angus MacDonald and the Reverend Archibald MacDonald, however, would have nothing to do with any concept of 'Celt versus Saxon/Teuton' promulgated by 'Scottish historians . . . blinded by race prejudice'. Any differences 'between Celtic and feudal Scotland' were just a matter of armament, although, surprisingly, they thought that Donald's 'kilted warriors' fought only with the 'claymore', 'protected by their wooden shields' against mail-clad 'Lowlanders' wielding metal shields.

That one side was of a higher culture than the other they thought was but 'a matter of opinion', and the fact that 'both sides fought with valour and determination . . . may well kindle the pride of Lowlander and Highlander alike'. 'The conflict, moreover, was not one between Celt and Saxon as such, nor was the struggle one for the supremacy of one race over the other'. It had simply been a 'struggle between kinsfolk' for power and land, between two first cousins, not 'between the opposing forces of civil order and barbarism'.

The Battle of Harlaw has been epitomised as a turning point in Scottish history: as finally deciding whether or not the Celts or the Saxons/Teutons should rule the country; as the beginning of the end for the Lordship of the Isles; as the stigmatisation of the Gaels as violent rebels against the state; as the alienation of Gaeldom from the Stewart kings; as the beginning of the end of Gaelic language and culture.

Whether or not any of these claims can be justified by calling on Donald's invasion of the territories of both 'Highlands' and 'Lowlands', ending in a battle in which on both sides a cousin of Gaelic origin, experienced in the commanding of Gaelic war bands, led men who were also speaking Gaelic, is another matter. It would seem that the disastrous result of family feud between two Scottish nobles, Donald of the Isles, and his uncle the Duke of Albany, Governor of Scotland and his house, is being asked to bear far too much significance.

Part 3

The Aftermath

10

Retreat and Abasement?

Only nightfall ended the battle, but although the sun had set at 8.30 p.m. on that Friday, 24 July (2 August in the modern calendar), the twilight extended for a good hour later. Mar's precipitous attack had deteriorated into a savage fight to the death, leaving a field of some three thousand dead, dying and wounded. A waxing moon would have done little to illuminate the scene, but morning light began to clear the darkness just after 3 am. Actual sunrise came an hour after, showing that Donald had managed to withdraw his entire army in those six hours of useful darkness. Hector Maclean's body had been carried away for burial at Iona, but of his fellow combatants, little is known for certain. As a chronicler vividly recounted: 'heir the bludie battel of the Harlaw was fochtine; gret slachter on baith handis, many alsweil knychtes as utheris nobles war na mair sein'.[1]

Donald may have only lost a fifth of his great army, and Mar – if the 'Highland' accounts are to be believed – was a commander severely wounded, as was the remaining half of his force. Why had Donald withdrawn and set off home? Whether or not driving an enormous force almost to Aberdeen had been a huge political bluff, or a glorified 'cattle raid' with the treasures of Aberdeen as a bonus, or had even been a combined operation with England, one thing was certain about the 'atrocious' battle that had resulted, expected or otherwise – it had turned out to be a serious mistake.

By nightfall Donald may still have had many thousands left in his army (although few would have escaped wounding and exhaustion), but he was now a hundred and sixty miles from Strome, the embarkation point for his Isles base, with an enraged countryside around him. There was every chance of his retreat being cut off, a retreat back through a ravaged region, with Forbes' forces easily able to come up through the Rhynie Gap and enfilade him at Huntly. With the likes of the Frasers and the Caithness men, to whom he had 'taught a lesson' when occupying Ross, potentially waiting for revenge, his position was precarious.

Worst of all, Donald had not only enabled the otherwise distrusted and disliked Governor Albany to raise the eastern nobility against him, a nobility whose near devastation now raised the spectre of countless blood feuds (despite any gentlemanly exchanging of memorial swords), but also the entire Scottish state could hardly ignore the horrendous bloodletting he had provoked at Harlaw. The Campbells for one might take the opportunity to displace Donald from his mainland territories. If he had hoped to demonstrate loyalty to James I by destabilising the Albany Stewarts, it would only be after James' return from England, and indeed, after Donald's death, that his family would be rewarded.

'The Lord of the Isles saw that nothing could be gained by pursuing the contest, and knowing that all Lowland Scotland was arrayed against him, he judged it the wisest policy to betake himself to the Isles.'[2] Thereafter, the 'Sleat historian' claimed: 'After the battle Macdonald returned again to the Isles, no opposition being made to him all his lifetime in Ross.'[3] Nothing could have been further from the sorry truth, for as Walter Bower described a few years later (Latin version in Appendix I):

> Immediately after the battle the duke of Albany as governor collected an army and approached the castle of Dingwall in Ross which belonged to the lord of the Isles by right of his wife. He took it over and arranged for its custody at the end of autumn. And the following summer he mobilised three forces/regiments to march against the lord of the Isles/named Donald, and his lands this side of the islands, to drive out his people from them.

Donald may have been invulnerable for a time in his Isles, but his people on his mainland holdings were not. That they were subsequently assailed might not have been unexpected, but the sheer size and ferocity of Albany's attack was another matter:

> The Lord of the Isles retreated, without molestation from the enemy, and was allowed to recruit his exhausted strength. As soon, however, as news of the disaster reached the ears of the Duke of Albany, then Regent of Scotland, he set about collecting

an army with which he marched in person to the north in the autumn, determined to bring the Lord of the Isles to obedience. Having taken possession of the Castle of Dingwall, he appointed a governor, and from thence proceeded to recover the whole of Ross.[4]

Albany, more renowned for cunning than physical aggression, had somehow managed to raise 'three armies' from the rest of Lowland Scotland, and to lead them in person, not only to strip Donald of possession of Ross, its principal castle of Dingwall, and his mainland territories, but also to bring him to heel and humiliate him. Raising such a force was an unexpected achievement, considering that the nobility as far down as the Tay had been shattered at Harlaw, but Donald – the most powerful magnate in Scotland, able to draw on reserves of many thousands of fighting men – had shown himself capable of rapidly destabilising the kingdom; he could hardly have been left triumphant with all his winnings, highly capable of attacking again. Albany may have been feared as a royal contender, but what had Donald's intentions been? No state could fail to suppress such a contestant, and the rest of Scotland appears to have responded.

The 'Sleat historian' gave a sinister explanation for Albany's action:

as long as the king was captive in England, the Duke of Albany the Regent used all his power to oppose him [Donald] and impair his greatness, being vexed that he lost the battle of Harlaw; and he and his son having an eye to the crown of Scotland, thought such a man as Macdonald might be a great hindrance to their designs and [that Donald] would not forsake the king [James I] his cousin on their account. Moreover, he was a man that would not be tainted or troubled with any hazardous or difficult enterprises . . . for any man that is well known and read in history, will know the king's [Robert II] issue were the greatest traitors and oppressors in the kingdom.[5]

The following year, 1412, Albany went further on the offensive:

Donald and his clansmen had retired to their Island strongholds. Within his own domains, the Island chief was impregnable, for his naval force was superior to the whole Scottish fleet at that time. He must, however, defend his mainland territories, and here the Regent, who determined to crush his power and humble the Island Lord, had his opportunity. In the following year, smarting from the humiliation and defeat at Harlaw, Albany resumed hostilities, proceeded at the head of an army to Argyle, and attacked Donald where alone he could do so with any chance of success.[6]

Abasement at Polgilb?

As to what happened next, Walter Bower, writing in the 1440s was quite certain.[7] Whether or not there was any actual fighting: 'Donald, for his personal safety hastened to him [Albany] at Polgilbe [Lochgilp] and provided sworn promises and hostages for keeping the peace and for compensating the king's subjects.'

Clan Donald historians, writing in the late nineteenth century, would have none of this.[8] They mistook the author of the above entry for 'that unreliable chronicler, John of Fordoun', stated that it was 'corroborated by no authority, whatever', that the records were obscure anyway, that Donald held his own, and that Albany was 'baffled in the effort to humble him'. Harlaw had resulted in 'well nigh the total anni-hilation of the Lowland army', with the Earl of Mar left covered in wounds. Why would Donald abase himself?

> The story of the treaty with the Governor at Polgilb, now Loch-gilp, where we find Donald coming forward humbly, laying down his assumed independence, consenting to become a vassal of the Scottish crown (which he was already – at least nominally), and delivering hostages for his future good behaviour, is given on the authority of that unreliable chronicler, John of Fordoun, and as he is corroborated by no authority, whatever, but, on the contrary, flatly contradicted by subsequent events, we refuse to receive it as anything but the purest fable. Such a treaty would have been looked upon an event of national importance, yet the national records are dumb regarding it.
>
> No contemporary chronicler, Highland or Lowland – if we omit John himself – records this successful termination of a rebellion so formidable as to have shaken the Scottish State to its very centre. Both in the Chamberlain and Exchequer Rolls we find references to the campaign of Albany against the Lord of the Isles in Argyle, but not the remotest reference is made to

the alleged treaty of Polgilb. What we find is the complaint made that the Governor had not been recouped for conveying an army to Polgilb against the Lord of the Isles, and for his expedition to Ross against the Caterans for the tranquillity of the realm.

If the Lord of the Isles, as John of Fordoun would have us believe, had surrendered at Polgilb and given hostages, the tone of the Scottish Chamberlain would have been more triumphant, and direst reference would have been made to such an important event. Donald well knew he could not take possession of the Earldom of Ross against all Scotland, and that he had resolved to make no further attempt in that direction his retreat from Harlaw clearly proves. His position in the Isles was too strong to be successfully attacked. Why, therefore, should he surrender at Polgilb? The fiction may be placed side by side with that other fable of the defeat, death, and burial of Donald at Harlaw, where his tomb is pointed out to this day!

Mar must have been very quick indeed to recover sufficiently from his reputed Harlaw injuries to take an active part in Albany's rapid response for which no expense was spared. Inverness had fallen quickly in the early stages of Donald's invasion and was not to be left so vulnerable again, as the Great Chamberlain accounts for 1412 and 1414 showed: [9]

> 1412. Payment is made to Lord Alexander, Earl of Mar, for various labours and expenses incurred in the war against the Lord of the Isles for the utility of the whole kingdom of £122 7s. 4d. ; and also to him for the construction of a fortalice at Inverness, for the utility of the kingdom, against said Lord of the Isles, £100; and for lime to Inverness for the construction of said fortalice, and for food and carriage of wood, £32 10s. 3d.

> 1414. Payment is made to Lord Alexander, Earl of Mar, in consideration of his divers labours and expenses about the castle of Inverness, of £52 11s. 3d.

Although it must be said that by 1415, the Exchequer Rolls did contain a complaint: 'And be it remembered, that the duke, the kingdom's governor did not receive the allowance . . . for the expenses of his army firstly at Polgilb against the lord of the Isles, and another time at Ross, for the kingdom's pacification of the katerans.' [10]

Furthermore, according to Boece, writing in Latin in 1527 (Appendix I), all this activity appears to have had the desired result: 'The Governor in the following year, with a strong army, preparing to attack the Hebrides, received Donald, petitioning for forgiveness, promising to make good all the losses caused, and swearing that he would never thereafter commit any injurious act, into favour.'[11]

Bellenden, writing in Scots for James V four years later, agreed with Boece:

> Donald disconnfist on this maner, past with grete diligence the samyn nycht to Ross, and efter that fled in the Ilis. Nochttheles, Duke Robert come sone eftir with ane grete army in the Ilis, quhaire Donald come to his will, and sworn nevir to invayd the realme agane with ony iniuris.[12]

The view held by the Gaels that Donald had effectively won the Battle of Harlaw is understandable. He still had a great functional army, whereas the remainder (half?) of Mar's forces were unfit for further combat. There also can be little doubt that had Donald chosen to remain offshore in his island kingdom he would have been unassailable, at least for the time being. But that would have left his mainland possessions vulnerable. Albany demonstrated just how vulnerable by his mustering of 'three armies' for a rapid repossession of Ross and his back-up fortification of both Dingwall and Inverness; an operation, furthermore, involving an Earl of Mar, who was anything but out of the game.

Abercromby in 1715, however, seemed to agree with the Gaels:

> while Donald, being rather wearied with Action, rather than conquered by Force of Arms, thought fit to retreat, first to Ross, then to the Isles; which he effected without any considerable Molestation, by reason that the shattered Forces in the North were not in a condition to pursue him, and those expected from the South and West were not yet come up. The petty War which was carried on at the same time against England no doubt retarded the Motion of these last and hindered the Governor from acting with that Vigour that was necessary, either against the domestic Rebels (for so he and the Bulk of the Nation called the Lord of the Isles and his Adherents,) or the foreign Enemies of the Kingdom: Yet he, or, which is the same thing, his Lieutenants, gained considerable advantages over both.[13]

Did Donald put up any resistance to Albany's forces on the mainland? Was there any fighting, and if so, where? 'Donald retreated before him, and took up his winter quarters in the Isles. Hostilities were renewed next summer [1412], but the contest was not long or doubtful – notwithstanding some little advantages obtained by the Lord of the Isles . . . '[14]

> He [Donald] must, however, defend his mainland territories, and here the Regent, who determined to crush his power and humble the Island Lord, had his opportunity.[15] In the following year, smarting from the humiliation and defeat at Harlaw, Albany resumed hostilities, proceeded at the head of an army to Argyle, and attacked Donald where alone he could do so with any chance of success. The records of the period are very obscure as to the fortunes and reverses alike of the Regent's campaign against the hero of Harlaw, but subsequent events indicate very clearly that Donald held his own, and that Albany was baffled in the effort to humble him.

Any fighting would seem to have been brief, and a compromise appears to have been effected at Lochgilphead, at the junction with Campbell territory – probably as far as Donald would be prepared to go. Was he completely humiliated there, 'compelled to give up his claim to the Earldom of Ross, to become a vassal to the Scottish crown, and to deliver hostages to secure his future good behaviour',[16] as well as 'providing compensation for the king's subjects'?[17] In 1597, however, Leslie maintained that 'in a schort space he was in fauour with the gouernour';[18] The Forbes family 'Memoirs' two hundred years later also asserted that following Donald's retreat to the Isles, he 'was shortly after reconciled to the Governour.'[19]

By such a reconciliation another bloody battle had thus been avoided, but if Donald had indeed 'won the close-fought battle of Harlaw', what had he gained from it? The gratitude of Henry IV for taking the threat of invasions off England? The goodwill of the captive James I for a serious attempt to destabilise the usurping Albany and family? A demonstration that he was the most powerful magnate in Scotland both by sea and by land, capable of bringing great battle-hardened forces into the field? But his violent thrust into mainland Scotland had in the end gained him neither the lands nor the Earldom of Ross. The atrociously bloody battle he had provoked had decimated the nobility of the North-East and East of Scotland, giving rise to a potential array of blood feuds, and had shocked the remainder sufficiently to rally behind the Duke of Albany in order both to recoup all of Donald's campaign gains and to threaten his mainland lands and people. Albany could not afford to have a perpetual threat from the west hanging over him.[20]

> Albany undoubtedly took possession of the Earldom of Ross, and prevented the Lord of the Isles from pushing his claim to that important inheritance; but Donald held undisputed sway to the day of his death within his own island principality. In no sense can Donald be said to have enjoyed the Earldom of Ross, save during those weeks when he invaded and occupied the district by force of arms. He never was, and never could be *de jure*, Earl of Ross. The Regent carried his point. In 1415, Euphemia resigned the earldom in favour of her grandfather [Albany], who thereafter conferred it on his son, John Stewart, Earl of Buchan.

Lastly, in the 1960s, Marion Campbell of Kilberry and Mary Sandeman, in their archaeological survey of Mid Argyll, described the following:

> 'Three boulders. each about 5 ft square, lying together between tidemarks on the E shore of Loch Gilp, below Kilmory', are traditionally described by three informants as 'witnesses' to the signing of the Treaty of Polgillip (between the Regent Albany and the Lord of the Isles in AD 1412).[21]

After spasmodic mainland forays, Donald appears to have turned thereafter to more peaceful matters:

> He (Donald) was one who kept clerics and priests and monks in his companionship, and he gave lands in Mull and in Isla to the monastery of Iona, and every immunity which the monastery of Iona had from his ancestors before him; and he made a covering of gold and silver for the relics of the hand of Columba, and he himself took the brotherhood of the order, having left a lawful and suitable heir in the sovereignty of the Isles and of Ross, viz., Alexander, son of Donald. He afterwards died in Isla, and was buried in the church of Odran [Iona].[22]

As will be seen, the fate of the Lordship itself had still to be played out.

The Fates of the Earldom of Mar and the Earldom of Ross/ Lordship of the Isles

The Earldom of Mar

As noted earlier, Alexander Stewart had gained his earldom by marrying Isabella, the widowed Countess of Mar. Nineteenth-century historians were to maintain the accusations that while her first husband Malcolm Drummond was engaged on building a tower in Kindrochit, in 1402 a band of ruffians led by Alexander seized Drummond and imprisoned him so cruelly that he died. Alexander then seized and married the widow and occupied Kildrummy Castle. In the summer of 1404, in an act of blatant hypocrisy, Alexander publicly returned the castle and its property to Isabella, who in turn resigned both to him, along with the Earldom of Mar and Lordship of the Garioch. A proposed charter stated that the Earldom and the rest of the Mar inheritance was to descend to any heirs produced by Alexander and Isabella (who was, however, not to survive another four years), whom failing, to Alexander's heirs. This was denied royal assent and in the late November a compromise allowed Alexander's marriage to Isabella and enjoyment of the life rent of Mar and Garioch, but if the marriage itself produced no heirs (as was to be the case), the Earldom was to pass the Isabella's nearest heirs.

Stephen Boardman does not accept the above accusations, stating that Alexander was entirely blameless in respect of Drummond's death and that his ceremony at Kildrummy was witnessed by a number of prominent local men, including Sir Andrew Leslie of Balquhain and Alexander Irvine of Drum, who were keen to see the son of the Wolf of Badenoch established as Earl of Mar. Albany had left the region without an active lord for too long, and it was 'Alexander's established ability to command and control cateran forces in the upland lordships to the west of Mar which made his protection and overlordship attractive and relevant to the lairds of the earldom and the Garioch.'[23]

In 1426, Alexander, wanting to retain the succession for his own heir, the illegitimate Thomas, cleverly resigned the Earldom to the Crown, to receive it back by a charter granting it to himself for life and to his heirs. If there were none, the Earldom was to revert to the Crown. Unfortunately for these plans, Thomas died without children before Alexander's own death in 1435, and the king, James I, whose determined policy was 'to break up, destroy and annex to the Crown the great feudal or feudalised Earldoms of Scotland . . . by devolution to the Crown', brushed aside the claims of any of Isabella's heirs. The Earldom of Mar was annexed to the Crown.[24]

The Earldom of Ross/the Lordship of the Isles

The fates of the Earldom of Ross and that of Clan Donald were to remain interlinked for over eighty years, throughout the lifetimes of two more Lords of the Isles determined to hold on to their independence, and of three king James of Scotland, equally determined to bring Scotland's earldoms under the Crown.

A great compression of historical events delivers the following simplified account. Regardless of any claim to be 'earl of Ross' (which the stalemated Donald might still make until his death in 1423), when poor Euphemia resigned Ross in 1415, the Duke of Albany, as 'Lord of the ward of Ross' (a post he had assumed back in 1405), gave the Earldom to his second son, John, Earl of Buchan.[25] John, however, was to perish in a resumption of the Hundred Years War, when the Scottish army he had led to support France was annihilated at Verneuil in 1424, and the Earldom passed next to John's son Robert, and thereafter to the Crown.

From as early as 1427, Donald's son Alexander had been titling himself '[3rd] lord of the Isles and master of the earldom of Ross'; he controlled Inverness, and was exercising a strong influence as far east as Badenoch and the Moray coast. It is noteworthy that he had been placed on King James' Stirling assize that condemned the Duke of Albany's family to death in 1425; the Government recognised his dominance by appointing him to the justiciarship that the Stewarts of Badenoch once held and which the Crown had since annexed. The tables had turned. The Earldom of Mar was in the hands of the Crown; Clan Donald once again effectively held the Earldom of Ross.

The following years, however, were eventful for Alexander. He was arrested by James I along with other Highland chiefs at a gathering in Inverness but managed to escape. He gathered his forces, burned Inverness, but wisely surrendered when faced with a royal army at Lochaber and underwent a humiliating submission at Edinburgh in 1429, 'clad only in shirt and drawers'. The queen and important lords apparently interceded on behalf of the supplicant and he was merely imprisoned in Tantallon Castle.[26] His cousins, however, successfully carried on the rebellion and defeated the royal army at Inverlochy in 1431. Alexander was released to pursue a lawful life thereafter, cooperating with the Crown – although with varying loyalty – as the fully established 'twelfth earl of Ross' in 1436, administering the lordship and earldom as a single unit with one council.

Alexander died in 1449. His son John succeeded him as 4th Lord of the Isles and 13th Earl of Ross, but joined an exiled Earl of Douglas in a treaty with Edward IV of England by which the two earls – though as vassals of Edward – would divide Scotland between them (the so-called treaty of Westminster-Ardtornish). But when James III finalised a fifteen-year truce with England with a peace treaty in 1474, he was enraged to discover the plot, and John was summoned for treason and found guilty in his absence the following year.[27] His estates were forfeited, and the Earldom of Ross was annexed to the Crown. By renouncing his claim to the Earldom and his other positions, however, within two years he was pardoned and reinstated, to retain an uneasy hold on the Lordship of the Isles.

John's only son Angus Og rebelled against him with the support of Clan Donald. Although after a sea battle they were reconciled, he died before his father. Angus's illegitimate son Dòmhnall Dubh vainly made claim to the Lordship before disappearing to die in Ireland in 1545. John was unable to control his people, and after a further rebellion by a nephew, he surrendered the Lordship of the Isles to the Crown in 1493, dying in Dundee in 1503 as a pensioner of the royal court.

Thus in just over eighty years from the Battle of Harlaw, the Earldoms of Mar and Ross were both absorbed by the Crown, and the Lordship of the Isles was forfeited.

11

Conclusions

It is now time to stand back from all these pages of written evidence to ask a number of questions.

Why did the Lord of the Isles choose the summer of 1411 to invade mainland Scotland? There would appear to be many possible reasons for such an invasion but no evidence as to why that particular summer was chosen.

How long did it take Donald to mobilise his force, which meant summoning fighting men from his widespread island and mainland kingdom, as well as from Ireland? Was this long enough for Albany and Mar to drum up resistance from Caithness to the Tay?

Was this resistance merely a hastily gathered, small, scratch army of some one thousand knights (although heavily armoured), which was rushed into forward defence of Aberdeen at Inverurie? There are *no* contemporary accounts of the size, composition and armament of Mar's force.

It is most unfortunate that there appear to be no contemporary written 'Highland' accounts of the battle and only one short account in actual Gaelic (mistranslated until now), but why did other accounts not appear until many centuries after the battle? Why did the Gaels claim the battle was a victory?

Indeed, why did Lowland histories, offering highly detailed descriptions of a careful controlled battle, its combatants and formations, also only appear some three hundred years after Harlaw? Why did they ignore an early account of chaos and incompetence? Why did these later Lowland historians depict Harlaw as a sound defeat for Donald when none of the Latin chroniclers had come to that conclusion?

Given that these later Lowland histories detail all the knights and nobles who came from the North-East of Scotland to join Mar, why did the Latin accounts list none of them as either being present or killed, other than Irvine of Drum and Provost Davidson?

Why did they not mention Forbes as taking part in the fighting? Why was a ballad depicting him (and a brother) as the sole hero of the battle (and slaying Donald into the bargain) composed in the late eighteenth century?

Lastly, what are the 'realities' concerning the battle, if the mediaeval accounts may be so described? Did Donald's invasion simply deteriorate into a glorified *chevauchée*, a destructive 'cattle raid' that went hideously wrong? Why would a powerful magnate, secure in his lands and titles, make such a gamble and antagonise both friends and enemies?

Why were detailed and romantic 'myths' elaborated by historians three or more centuries later, and why do they depict the battle as a racial 'Celt v. Saxon/Teuton' struggle for mastery of Scotland? Or of the triumph of 'civilisation' over 'barbarism'?

Possible Reasons for Donald's Invasion in the Summer of 1411

No contemporary 'Highland' prose accounts appear to have survived. If we examine the Lowland Latin histories, there are only two which were written down within years of the battle – Bower's *Scotichronicon* around 1440 and a single sentence in the *Book of Pluscarden* in 1461. The latter simply says that there was a battle at Harlaw between Donald and the Earl of Mar in which many nobles lost their lives, and gives no reasons for the conflict. Bower, however, is adamant that it was simply a 'crushing and pillaging' expedition with the dual aims of sacking Aberdeen, and taking control 'down to the river Tay'.

When we come to the Latin accounts written during the following century and seemingly still fresh in people's minds, John Mair in 1521 agreed that it was simply aimed at 'the spoiling of Aberdeen, a town of mark, and other places' by Donald's 'Wild Scots'. A few years later, in 1527, Boece began to elaborate. He accepted that Donald had made a valid claim to the Governor for what rumour seems to have said was a vacant Earldom of Ross (the only chronicler to mention his claim to the actual earldom as well as the territory), but had received a reply that contained 'nothing that was satisfactory to him'. Although he 'justly' and easily brought Ross under his control 'as the rightful heir', these chroniclers stated that wasn't enough for him and he then began to exhibit 'aggressive behaviour', driving out the peoples of the countryside as far down as Moray, Strathbogie, and then the Garioch, and threatening to despoil Aberdeen – a just claim and occupation of Ross, but followed by unjustified, belligerent behaviour.

By 1582, Buchanan recounted much the same story, although in his version the Governor had already illegally taken Ross-shire from Donald, who was indubitably 'the rightful heir', before giving him 'no satisfaction' for that wrong. Donald in turn invaded the mainland. He easily took possession of Ross, with the approval and compliance of the inhabitants, but that ease 'drove his mind, which was eager for plunder, to attempt more ambitious schemes'. These included bringing Moray 'under his own sway', pillaging Strathbogie, and threatening Aberdeen. Once again, the ease and approval of a justified occupation of Ross was seen as triggering Donald's aggression and a latent desire for plunder.

Although Gaels will eventually express their scorn for both Boece and Buchanan, 'partial pickers of Scotish chronology and history [who] never spoke a favourable word of the Highlanders, much less of the Islanders and Macdonalds', their versions of the battle's outcome will take over two hundred and fifty years to appear, thanks to the destruction of contemporary records.[1] Only the contemporary Irish accounts mentioned the battle – as a victory – but gave no reasons why Donald provoked it in the first place.

When it comes to the very much later 'second set' of histories from both Lowlands and 'Highlands' which appeared in the eighteenth and nineteenth centuries, additional causes for the invasion now begin to be proposed, for, although the Latin chroniclers had portrayed Donald as having a good legal right to Ross and the Earldom (Boece), justifying his occupation of the territory, they had decried his subsequent aggression and fear-inducing invasion 'in such large and savage numbers like locusts'. It was this aggression – especially Mair's depiction of 'wild Scots' fighting against 'civilised Scots' – that the later Lowland historians latched on to and elaborated. To Walter Scott and those who followed him this was the real nub of the matter – the everpresent, latent desire of the Celts to take over Scotland from the noble Saxons had been behind Donald's great invasion. Nothing less than wearing the Crown would do for Donald and his kin.

Although records are few, by over four hundred and fifty years after Harlaw, the 'Highland' views also appear settled. Donald, the rightful heir to the Earldom, had been provoked into action by a highly aggressive duke of Albany who wanted the Crown for himself, leaving James I to rot in England.[2] Donald had fought a decisive battle, made his point, spared Aberdeen, and returned home to a peaceful, Christian existence, unmolested for the remainder of his life. Any idea that the affair had been driven by racial hatred, or a desire for a Celtic takeover of Scotland, or even a treacherous, combined operation with England, was described as being absolute nonsense.

Inauguration of the Harlaw Monument

Five hundred years after the battle, the citizens of Aberdeen commissioned a great, stark tower on the battlefield as a monument to Provost Davidson and the Aberdeen burgesses who had died with him at Harlaw. It was inaugurated on 24 July 1914, at an event presided over by the Lord Provost Adam Maitland, a descendant of the family who had farmed Harlaw since the time of the battle, and whose ancestor 'had left the plough to take part'.[3]

William Mackay, an eminent Celtic scholar and authority on Highland history, one of the founders of the Gaelic Society of Inverness, and some time president of *An Comunn Gaidhealach*, made the principal address.[4] He summed up the evolution of both Highland and Lowland views of the battle over the centuries in a revisionist account which surprised those North-East folk who thought they had come to celebrate the deliverance of Aberdeen from a Highland horde of savages by an severely outnumbered army led by the noble Earl of Mar and their Provost.

After a detailed and lengthy development, Dr Mackay made a number of crucial points about the battle, which were later included in an address made to the Gaelic Society of Inverness. Firstly, he maintained, the contest was not one between Highland and Islands, or between Celt and Saxon. Donald's army was indeed composed of Norse-Gaels, but many of the followers of Mar (himself a Gael by birth and upbringing) and his people were Celts, Gaelic speakers. Nor was it a conflict between civilisation and barbarism – the Earl of Mar as a rough, wild leader of Gaelic war bands, who had gained his title underhandedly, contrasted with Donald of Isla, the most cultured Scottish chief of the day, a generous supporter of the Church, ever welcome at the English court, and an Oxford graduate [this last was untrue, unfortunately, as we now know].

Mar's Government army, furthermore, had not been a hastily summoned scratch force rushed into forward defence at Inverurie – there had been plenty time not only for the Celts of northern Scotland to mobilise against Donald, but also for a substantial army of knights and nobles to be gathered from the Spey to the Tay. [Although it should be noted that years later, in 1429, James I was able to muster all the Lowland nobility and attack a similar army of ten thousand men from Ross and the Isles in under three months.][5] Mar's army must easily have matched Donald's for size, and probably even outnumbered it. Donald had not rebelled against the king, but had invaded to rescue, from a rapacious Duke of Albany, the Earldom of Ross and its lands which extended as far down as Kincardine. There would have been no intention to sack Aberdeen (unless the city resisted).

Lastly, Donald had decisively won the Battle of Harlaw (although here Mackay quoted the mistranslated *Books of Clanranald* account that he merely 'fought' it). He withdrew in the knowledge that after such horrendous loss of life, 'all Scotland' would be against him – and his men would have wanted, anyway, to get home for the harvest. Bards such as MacCodrum, Iain Lom, Mairearad ni' Lachuinn, Iain MacAilein, Allan Macdougall and Archibald Grant had alluded to the battle, enthusiastically confident in the general view that 'the Macdonalds and their allies had undoubted victory on the gory field of Harlaw'.

One interesting result of this measured address was the confession then made at the ceremony by the Convener of Aberdeenshire, a Mr Duff of Hatton, in his toast to 'the Memory of Provost Davidson and the Heroes of Harlaw'. He had come to the occasion, he said, 'brought up in the old fashioned and erroneous nation that at the battle of Harlaw there was a fight for a principle between two civilisations'. He now accepted that there was no historical foundation for the view that the war was a struggle for mastery between the Highlands and Lowlands, between the Celts and the Saxons, or between barbarism and civilisation, but that it was purely a family feud between Donald of the Isles and his uncle the Duke of Albany, Regent of Scotland, and his house. 'For the errors which have spread on this and other points, Sir Walter Scott and Mr Fraser-Tytler, the Historian of Scotland, are greatly responsible', he complained.

Duff proceeded to disprove these errors in great detail, quoting the misconceptions of the many historians who had followed Scott. He now realised that the battle was no 'final struggle for supremacy', there was no 'Highland avalanche' engulfing Mar's 'little army', no attempts by 'representatives of the Norse race' to extend their island empire into an independent monarchy as far as the border with England, with the sacking of Aberdeen as a bonus on the way. Whether those who thought they had come to inaugurate a monument to the brave defenders of Aberdeen were as convinced remains a moot point, but Duff at least demolished the Romantic nonsense of Scott and his followers.

But before finally returning to the fundamental question – why Donald took such a great gamble – it might be too soon to dismiss these very late 'histories' of the battle as speculative and imagined accounts, and to 'try, instead of picturing fancy scenes, to explain the motive of the battle and its significance for the country instead', in the sensible words of Aberdeen's Professor of Logic, William Davidson, at the above ceremony. Nevertheless, at the 600th anniversary of the battle, held around the monument, on 14 July 2011, the Gaelic *Brosnachadh* was read out, the descendants of the families of Irvine of Drum and Maclean of Duart shook hands in reconciliation, and there was a film shown later in Inverurie Academy of a pageant of schoolchildren enacting the battle, singing the 'Forbes ballad' and marching as the North-East noble families, emblazoned shields and banners flying.

Colourful heraldic shields had finally been placed on the empty bosses on the monument (there had been insufficient funds to provide these back in 1914), not just those of Provost Robert Davidson and of the Royal Burgh of Aberdeen (for the Burgesses), but four more, generously representing the noble invaders, Donald, Lord of the Isles, and Sir Hector Maclean of Duart, as well as defenders, the Earl of Mar and Sir Alexander Irvine of Drum. Notably missing was any representation of the families of Leslie or Forbes.

Barbarism versus Civilisation?

When dealing with later 'Highland' histories, it is perhaps unfair to harp on how few there are. Accounts and records of the Lords of the Isles especially are known to have been destroyed after the break-up of their realm, and any tradition of prose recording may have faltered for many years thereafter in what was a predominately oral culture. The first serious 'Highland' historian, Donald Gregory, dismissed the battle in his 1881 *History of the Western Highlands and Isles of Scotland* as being 'too well known to require repetition'.[6]

The likes of the 'Sleat historian' clearly had a mission to undo the denigration of the Macdonalds by the Latin chroniclers but why was such a riposte delayed until the Lordship was centuries past, until the overthrow of James VII and the ascent of William of Orange? The late seventeenth century onwards 'saw a pronounced surge in antiquarian, collecting and publishing endeavours in the Scottish *Gàidhealtachd* in respect of literary, ethnographical and linguistic studies', for reasons that were very many and complex.[7] One factor was the centralising of the Scottish state – titles and lands had to be justified in Scots law, in English, and in Edinburgh, and their origins and histories examined in the process.[8] The Highlands, and especially the Macdonalds, were to pay a heavy price for supporting the last of the Stewart line during the Risings; afterwards it is unsurprising that attempts should be made to relate and record their great histories and achievements.

To consider the reason for the contents and timing of Lowland historians who followed Scott and Tytler is to enter further into the uncertain world of historical speculation, but it is difficult to ignore that they circled around the Jacobite Risings. The 'Wild Scots' from the west had once more appeared in frightening array; describing how they were checked by the Battle of Harlaw might help to reassure a nervous British Government (which had recently expended consider-able sums in opening up the road systems so that troops might rapidly quell any further rebellions) that they would never do so again. Had not a previous horde been heroically stalemated by noble 'Saxon' defenders? All speculation, with which not all historians would agree: the 'final expiration [of the Lordship] in the person of Dòmhnall Dubh in 1545 makes for perhaps over-seductive symmetry with the begin-ning of the end of Jacobitism exactly two centuries later'.[9]

The creation of the 'Forbes ballad' in the late 1700s, though, may have been a case in point, perhaps explaining why, post Culloden, it was thought valuable or even necessary to portray Lord Forbes and a brother as the sole defenders of Lowland Scotland against a huge horde of savage Highlanders. As already noted, over in the North-East, Alexander Forbes, 4th Lord Pitsligo, although from a Whig family, had taken part in the Risings of both 1715 and 1745. His estates were forfeited but he managed to hide on his own lands until his death in 1762. If the ballad was indeed intended to help restore his family's fortunes (and perhaps portray it as a bulwark against incursions of wild men from the west), it was unsuccessful, for on the death of his son the title became dormant.[10]

Finally, it may be important to address the 'second set' of Lowland claims that there was a considerable Highland/Lowland divide, which Donald had crossed, leading his 'Wild Scots', for had not Mair also thus described them back in 1521? And what of their 'monstrous savagery' Buchanan later said they exhibited? Whatever the history of any 'Great Ill-Will' described as held by the Lowlanders against the Gaels, both before and after Harlaw, any such racial and cultural antipathy does not seem to have been a factor in that actual conflict.[11]

Albany's position as governor or guardian of the kingdom for much of the period between 1388 and his death in 1420 meant that a figure with extensive interests inside Gaelic Scotland continued to direct the affairs of the Crown. If the 'Great Ill-Will of the Lowlander' was a significant cultural and political force in early Stewart Scotland, then it hardly seems a phenomenon that was actively promoted and encouraged by those who wielded royal power between 1371 and 1424:

> The return of James I to Scotland in 1424 and his subsequent destruction of the Albany family may have marked a significant shift in the relationship between the Stewart dynasty and Gaelic Scotland, but this case remains to be made rather than assumed. The emergence after 1424 of a more active, aggressive and ambitious style of kingship was allied to the waning of the personal ties of residence and kinship that had bound Robert II and the Albany Stewarts to Gaelic Scotland. Moreover, James' innate suspicion of those areas associated with the Albany lordship was combined with an increasing emphasis on the projection of royal power through the imposition of uniform administrative, legal and bureaucratic systems on all the regions of the kingdom.

Had James I actually been on the throne when Donald invaded, the eventual outcome would have been the same, for no ruler of Scotland, especially the centralising Stewarts, could have put up with a magnate both able and willing to cause such an enormous disruption. That Donald's action could be (temporarily) taken as a support for an exiled king against a usurping Governor, and thus for the time being worthy of reward, would not hide the dangerous potential of Lords of the Isles to be capable of acting as petty kings, seeking their own interests and undertaking their own alliances, especially with England.

It is also highly limiting to see Donald's invasion as involving 'only' Ross and its eastern holdings, and affecting 'only' those involved both in attack and defence. With the Stewarts only relatively recently established on the throne of an independent country still in a state of flux and development, Donald's action, as he was eventually to realise, had turned the country as a whole against him, providing the Campbells for one with an opportunity to further usurp his lands and titles.[12] Displaying an ability to shatter any Government army which might attempt to thwart him was no way to win hearts and minds, provoking blood feuds, no matter how many chivalrous sword exchanges.

Donald's Gamble

The Battle of Harlaw has curiously faded from Scottish history – other than in the minds of the Aberdonians and their countryside – and is recalled largely via the 'second sets' of imaginative and often romantic stories written hundreds of years after the battle. When deciding which if any of these may be taken as 'real' histories of the battle it is as well to recall the honest assessment eventually confessed by the 1896 Clan Donald historians themselves:

> Trustworthy records of this famous fight there are none. Lowland historian and ballad composer, as well as Highland seanachie, described what they believed must and should have happened.[13]

And as an Irvine of Drum historian was later to bitterly complain, 'much has been written about that battle, and some of it is pure fiction'.[14]

Despite the strong objections that the likes of the earlier 'Sleat historian' made to the accounts given by mediaeval chroniclers, their succinct assessment of Donald's invasion, and the 'atrocious' battle it evoked, would yet seem the most likely. They had concurred that Donald had a good title to the Earldom and lands of Ross, and that he was provoked by the Duke of Albany's rejection into claiming them physically. They gave no clues as to the time it took to organise the invasion and whether or not starting it in the summer of 1411 was on a sudden impulse or long planned. (The rumours that the sickly Ross heiress was being forced into a nunnery, and thus 'out of the world' legally, will have started after Albany made her his ward back in 1405, yet Donald takes another ten years to invade and claim Ross physically.) But it was most unfortunate, they believed, that Donald's easy occupation of Ross, and his warm reception by its people as their rightful ruler, had deluded and triggered him into extending his occupation and control of Ross into those territories of the Earldom which extended across and down into the East of Scotland.

'Eager for plunder', they maintained, Donald and his men both terrified and looted the inhabitants of those territories on the way, with the firm intention of sacking the town of Aberdeen. He met with stubborn resistance on the plateau of Harlaw from a remarkable defence raised from between the Spey and the Tay (although the mystery remains why, other than Irvine of Drum, no North-East nobles are actually described), in a battle fought to the death, a battle unheard of in previous history for its frightful toll of dead and wounded, and from which Donald simply withdrew his army homewards that night. An 'atrocious' battle of which only one thing could be said with any certainty, as the later 'Forbes ballad' rightly concluded:

'You could scarce tell wha had won'

In other words, what might have been considered a justified action had developed into an unjust one. In demonstrating that he was the most powerful magnate in Scotland, capable of raising a huge army, Donald clearly made a serious misjudgement by invading the mainland, and by embarking thereafter on a rapid plundering and destructive raid, which in the wretched, ongoing Hundred Years War were known as *'chevauchées'*. The mediaeval chroniclers provided no evidence for any grand motive, no attempt to conquer and wrest control of all Scotland from the 'Saxons', no desire to wear its Crown, no combined operation with England, no attempt to destabilise the Duke of Albany on James I's behalf.

They provided no romantic battle descriptions of the fighting on either side, with North-East nobles especially, advancing in glorious order, banners flying, trumpets sounding; only a horrified description of a chaotic attack. Mar's reinforcement had been sent in disordered, piecemeal, resulting in unnecessary loss of lives. These chroniclers, writing for later Stewart kings, were indeed succinct but sure – the end result of Donald's impetuous invasion, on the blood-drenched plateau of Harlaw, was both inconclusive and atrocious.

Within the century, the Lordship had been assimilated by the Crown, as were the Earldoms of Ross and Mar. It would seem that the only 'winner' of the Battle of Harlaw – other than those relieved Aberdonians – was James, the prisoner-poet down in London, and his royal Stewart successors.

Appendix I

Latin Sources

1378. Richard II's Safe Conduct for Donald to Study at Oxford (Transcript)

Salvus conductus pro Donaldo, filio Johannis de Insulis, clerico.
Riccardus per terras suas patentes per sexcennium suscepit in salvum et securum conductum suum ac in protectionem et defensionem Riccardi septentrionales Donaldum filium Johannis de Out Isles in Scotia clericum veniendo in regnum Angliae per dominium et potestatem Riccardi tam per terram quam per mare usque villam Oxoniam ibidem in universitate studendo morando et exinde ad propria redeundo. Dum tamen idem Donaldus quicquam quod in regni Riccardi seu coronae suae praejudicum cedere possit non attemptet seu attemptare faciat quovis modo.

c.1440s. *Scotichronicon*, by Walter Bower

The Account of the Battle of Harlaw

Anno domini m ccc.xi in vigilia Sancti Jacobi apostoli conflictus de Harlaw in Marria ubi Donaldus de Ilis cum decem milibus de Insulanis et hominibus suis de Ross hostiliter intravit terram omnia conculcans et depopulans ac in vastitatem redigens, sperans in illa expedicione villam regiam de Abirdene spoilare et consequentur usque ad aquam de Thaia sue subicere dicioni. Et quia in tanta multitudine ferali occupaverunt terram sicut locuste, conturbati sunt omnes de dominica terra qui videbant eos et timuit omnis homo. Cui occurit Alexander Stewart comes de Mar cum Alexandro Ogilby vicecomite de Angus qui semper et ubique justiciam dilexit cum potestate de Angus et Mernez, et facto acerimo congressu occisis sunt ex parte comitis de

Mar Jacobus Scrimgeour, Alexander de Irewin, Robertus Malvile, Thomas Murrave milites, Willelmus de Abirnethi filius et heres domini de Salton, et nepos gubernatoris, Alexander Strayton dominus de Laurenston, Georgius de Ogilby heres domini eiusdem, Jacobus Lovale, Alexander de Strivelyne et alii valentes armigeri, necnon Robertus David consul de Abirdene cum multis burgensibus. De parte Insularum cecidit armidoctor Mclane nomine et dominus Dovenaldus capitaneus fugatus, et ex parte eius occisi nongenti et ultra. Ex parte nostra vc et fere omnes generosi de Buch-[ane].

Albany's Return with Three Armies

Incontinenti post bellum dux Albanie gubernator congregato exercitu accessit ad castrum de Dingvall (in Ross) quod fuit domini Insularum (ex parte uxoris sue). Et illud recepit eidem custodiam deput[avit] (in fine autumpni). Et in sequenti estate collegit tres exercitus ad invadendum dominum Insularum/dictum Dovenaldum et terras suas citra insulas ad depopulandum;

Donald at Polgilb

cui [idem/ipse Donaldus de assecurancia/ad securantia occur-]it apud Polgilbe et de pace conservanda at indempnitate regis juramenta et obsides [prestitit].

c.1461. *Liber Pluscardensis* ('*Book of Pluscarden*')
The Account of the Battle of Harlaw

Item anno Domini mccccxi fuit conflictus de Harlaw, in Le Gariach, per Donaldum de Insulis contra Alexandrum comitem de Mar et vice-comitem Angusiae, ubi multi nobiles ceciderunt in bello.

1521. *Historia Maioris Britanniae, tam Angli[a]e q[uam] Scoti[a]e*, by John Mair [or Major]
The Account of the Battle of Harlaw

Anno 1411, praelium Harlaw apus Scotos famigeratum commissum est. Donaldus insularum comes decies mille viris clarissimis sylvestribus Scotis munitus, Aberdoniam urbem insignem et alia loca spoilare proposuit: contra quem Alexander Steuartus comes Marrae, et Alexander Ogilvyus Angusiae vice-comes suos congregant, et Donaldo Insularum apud Harlaw occurrunt. Fit atrox et acerrima pugna; nec cum exteris praelium periculosius in tanto numero unquam habitum est; sic quod in schola grammaticali juvenculi ludentes, ad partes oppositas nos solemus retrahere, dicentes nos praelium de Harlaw struere velle. Licet communius a vulgo dicatur quod sylvestres Scoti erant victi, ab annalibus tamen oppositum invenio: solum Insularum comes coactus est retrocedere; et plures occisos habuit quam Scoti domiti: sed Donaldum non fugarunt; at viri temeritatum animosissime represserunt. Campiductorum eius Maklane occiderunt, cum aliis nongentis, pluribus autem pessime laesis. Sexcenti meridionalium solum interierunt, quorum aliqui erant viri nobiles, Guillelmus Abrenethyus primogenitus et haeres domini Saultoni, Georgius Ogilvius, eiusdem domini haeres, Jacobus Skrymgeourus, Alexander de Irvin, Robertus Malvile, Thomas Mures auriti equites, Jacobus Luval, Alexander Strevilinus cum quibusdam minoris famae nobilius. Sed quia paucissimi evaserunt non laesi, et diuturna erat pugna, atrox reputata est.

1527. *Scotorum Historia,* by Hector Boece

The Account of the Battle of Harlaw

At Donaldus qui amitam Eufemiae Alexandri Lesle sororem, uxorem habebat, ubi Eufemiam defunctam audivit, a gubernatore postulavit ex hereditate Rossiae comitatum: ubi quum ille nihil aequi respondisset, collecta ex Hebridibus ingenti manu partim vi, partim benevolentia, secum ducens, Rossiam invadit, nec magno negocio in ditionem suam redegit, Rossianis verum recipere haeredem haud quaquam recusantibus. Verum eo successu non contentus, nec se in eorum quae jure petiverat, finibus continens, Moraviam, Bogevallem, iisque vicinas regiones hostiliter depopulando in Gareotham pervenit, Aberdoniam, uti minitabatur, direpturus. Caeterum in tempore obvians temeritate eius, Alexander Stuart Alexandri filii Roberti regis secundi comitis Buthquhaniae nothus, Marriae comes ad Hairlau (vicus est pugna mox ibi gesta cruentissima insignis) haud expectatis reliquis auxiliis cum eo congressus est. Qua re factum est, ut dum auxilia sine ordinibus (nihil tale suspicantes) cum magna negligentia advenirent, permulti eorum caesi sint, adeoque ambigua fuerit victoria, ut utrique se in proximos montes desertis castris victoria cedentes receperint. Nongenti ex Hebridianis et iis qui Donaldo adhaeserant cecidere cum Makgillane et Maktothe, praecipuis post Donaldum ducibus. Ex Scotis adversae partis vir nobilis Alexander Ogilvy Angusiae vicecomes, singulari justitia ac probitate praeditus, Jacobus Strimger, Comestabulis Deidoni, magno animo vir ac insigni virtuti, et ad posteros clarus, Alexander Irrvein a Drum ob praecipium robur conspicuus, Robertus Maul a Panmoir, Thomas Moravus, Wilhelmus Abernethi a Salthon, Alexander Strathon a Loucenstoun, Robertus Davidstoun, Aberdoniae praefectus: hi omnes equites aurati cum multis aliis nobilibus eo praelio occubuere. Donaldus victoriam hostibus prorsus concedens, tota nocte quanta potuit celeritate ad Rossiam contendit, ac inde qua proxime dabatur, in Hebrides se recepit.

Donald, Petitioning for Forgiveness at Lochgilp

Gubernator insequenti anno cum valido exercitu Hebrides oppugnare parans Donaldum veniam supplicantem, ac omnia praestiturum damna illata pollicentem, nec deinceps iniuria vllam illaturum iurantem in gratiam recepit.

1582. *Rerum Scoticarum Historia,* by George Buchanan

The Account of the Battle of Harlaw

Altero vero post anno, qui fuit a Christo 1411, Donaldus Insulanus Aebudarum dominus cum Rossiam iuris calumnia per Gubernatorem sibi ablatam, velut proximus haeres (uti erat) repeteret, ac nihil aequi impetraret, collectis insulanorum decem millibus in continentem descendit: ac Rossiam facile occupauit, cunctis libenter ad iusti domini imperium redeuntibus. Sed ea Rossianorum parendi facilitas animum praedae auidum ad maiora audenda impulit. In Moraviam transgressus eam praesidio destitutam statim in suam potestatem redegit. Deinde Bogiam praedabundus transiuit: et iam Abredoniae imminebat. Adversus hunc subitum, et inexpectatum hostem Gubernator copias parabat: sed cum magnitudo, et propinquitas periculi auxilia longinqua expectare non sineret, Alexander Marriae

Comes ex Alexandro Gubernatoris fratre genitus cum tota ferme nobilitate trans Taum ad Harlaum vicum ei se obiecit. Fit praelium inter pauca cruentum et memorabile: nobilium hominum virtute de omnibus fortunis, deque gloria adversus immanem feritatem decertante. Nox eos diremit magis pugnando lassos, quam in alteram partem re inclinata adeoque incertus fuit eius pugnae exitus, ut utrique cum recensuissent, quos viros amisissent, sese pro victis gesserint. Hoc enim praelio tot homines genere, factisque clari desiderati sunt, quos vix ullus adversus exteros conflictus per multos annos absumpsisse memoratur. Itaque vicus ante obscurus ex eo ad posteritatem nobilitatus est.

Appendix II

The Orthography of the 'Ramsay ballad'

The orthography of the 'Ramsay ballad' is a partly modernised and occasionally Anglicised Older Scots, nowhere incorrect as such. Typical Older Scots spellings include <quh>; <sch>; final <e> in *se* and *Dunde*; <oi> in *befoir*; final <ill> in *battill*; and hypercorrect <ing> in *Irving*. The tailed z (yogh) appears in its printed form as <z>, e.g. *Zit*. There are only a few vestiges (such as we might expect in the second half of the sixteenth century) of earlier spellings such as the present participle ending in -*and*, and <oi> for <ui> (*behoif*). The redundant <t> in <cht> (*thocht* 'though', stanza XXI) had almost disappeared by c.1570.

Also curious is the spelling *meint* 'meant' (stanza II). Modern dialects differ in whether they have /t/ or /d/ for this suffix after nasals (and likewise after /r/ and /l/). The word rhymes with *freind*, so a spelling in <d> would have been expected, especially as similar words in the text have <d> (*langd*, *kend*, *spaird*). This suggests that the *meint* spelling is original, not something introduced by Ramsay – if concocting a period piece, why choose a spelling that contradicts both the rhyme and the dialect suggested by other forms in the text?

Many word-forms are again convincingly Older Scots, in particular final <f> rather than <v> in *gaif*, *haif*, etc.; *quaint* 'acquainted'; *chiftain*; *togither*; *chessit* 'chased'; and *semblit* 'assembled', though the last reappears (whether as a new formation, or because of a gap in the record) in some twentieth-century dialects. However, *allangst* (stanza I) is not attested until Modern Scots (the Older Scots is *alangs*).

Two word forms suggest a date after the middle of the sixteenth century. *Not* (if original rather than a modernisation) points to a date after c.1560, while *quat* infinitive (stanza V) is attested from the 1590s onwards. However, neither of these is in rhyme, so need not be original.

The morphology is again partly modernised: *these* is uncommon before the seventeenth century, and *deirs* (plural of *deer*) is also modern. *A Dictionary of the Older Scottish Tongue* has a seventeenth-century example, and *The Oxford English Dictionary* knows it occasionally from the eighteenth century on. (It is also possible that the <s> here is a miscopied <e> – see below.)

There are two constructions that seem unidiomatic in Modern Scots, though are good Older Scots: the bare infinitive in *'promist . . . mak them men of mekle micht'* (stanza X) and the adjective *likelie* used absolutely, as a noun (stanza XXX).

The idiom and vocabulary is convincingly Older Scots, e.g. *frae hand* (stanza VI), *bandown* (stanza VII), *all and sum* (stanzas XV, XXVIII), *to the deid* (stanza XXIV), and *schene* (stanzas XV, XXIX), an Older Scots poetic term. An exception is *mony a ane* (stanza XXXI) where Older Scots would have *mony ane* – but the scansion suggests that *mony ane* is the correct reading.

As noted, Child found the rhymes 'artificial'. In practice, they are almost all perfect if read as Older Scots, apart from one or two awkward personal names. For *meint* (stanza II) read *meind*. For *fiery fairy* (stanza II) read *feery-farry*; this is first attested in 1529. For *quaint* (stanza III) read *quent*. For *aware* (stanza XIII) read *awar*. *Rewaird* (stanza XXIII) is a genuine form. For *bruik* (stanza XVIII) read *breuk* (as in *heuk*, etc.).

The rhyme *bene:dens* (stanza XXIII) suggests a miscopied <e>. If the word is *dene*, this would be 'a dingle', rather than 'an animal's lair' (*den*).

The following rhymes are suggestive of a date before 1600:

impatient:omnipotent (stanza V), which seems to require four
   syllables in *impatient*;
was:Angus (stanza XXVI) which implies /s/ not /z/ in *was*;
principall:all:small:fall (stanza XIV) – the conservative rhyme with
   /l/ in *all* etc. continued in Middle Scots, though the /l/ would have
   been lost in stressed syllables in most dialects.

Also notable is *throuch:Garioch* (stanza I). *Throuch* is not a feature of eighteenth-century literary Scots, though it must have survived into the seventeenth century in Central Scots, as it turns up in modern Ulster dialect. The only other modern dialect that preserves it, interestingly, is Aberdeenshire.

We may conclude that where the language deviates from Ramsay's eighteenth-century Scots, it is perfectly convincing as the reflection of an underlying pre-1600 text, as Ramsay claims. Particularly authentic touches are the spelling *meint* and the word forms, idioms, lexical items and rhymes mentioned above. We may suspect that Ramsay has misread a couple of <e> letters as <s> (*dens* and possibly *deirs*), which would suggest that he had a manuscript written in secretary hand in front of him, a style of writing that was used from the early sixteenth until the mid seventeenth century.

Notes

1. Introduction

1 Olson, I. A., 'Contemporary Scottish Music and Song: An introduction', in Zenzinger, P. (ed.), *Scotland: Literature, culture, politics* (Heidelberg: Carl Winter, 1989), pp. 139–66. See also Donaldson, W., 'Bonny Highland Laddie: The making of a myth', *Scottish Literary Journal* 3:2 (1976), pp. 30–50.

2 Wedderburn, R., *The Complaynt of Scotland (c. 1550)* (Edinburgh: Scottish Text Society, 1979), pp. 50–1.

3 Purser, J., *Scotland's Music* (Edinburgh and London: Mainstream, 2007), pp. 84–8. See also Bronson, B. H. (ed.), 'The Battle of Harlaw', in *The Traditional Tunes of the Child Ballads*, 4 vols (Princeton, New Jersey: Princeton University Press, 1959–72), III, pp. 117–25.

4 McLeod, W. and Bateman, M., *Duanaire na Sracaire: Songbook of the Pillagers: Anthology of Scotland's Gaelic verse to 1600* (Edinburgh: Birlinn, 2007), pp. 229–33, at pp. 230–1.

5 Mackay, W., 'The Battle of Harlaw: Its true place in Scottish history', *Transactions of the Gaelic Society of Inverness* 30 (1922), pp. 267–85, at p. 285.

6 See Appendix II.

7 Olson, I. A., 'The Battle of Harlaw, its Lowland Histories and their Balladry: Historical confirmation or confabulation?', *Review of Scottish Culture* 24 (2012), pp. 1–33.

2. The Opponents: The Lord of the Isles and the Earl of Mar

1 Munro, J. and Munro, R. W., *Acts of the Lords of the Isles 1336–1493* (Edinburgh: Blackwood, Pillans and Wilson, 1986), pp. xxix–xxxvi.

2 Oram, R., 'The Lordship of the Isles: 1336–1545', in Oman, D. (ed.), *The Argyll Book* (Edinburgh: Birlinn, 2004), p. 132.

3 Bannerman, J., 'The Lordship of the Isles', in Brown, J. M. (ed.), *Scottish Society in the Fifteenth Century* (London: Edward Arnold, 1977), pp. 211–16.

4 Paul, J. B. (ed.), 'MacDonald, Lord of the Isles', in *The Scots Peerage: Founded on Wood's edition of Sir Robert Douglas's peerage of Scotland: Containing an historical and genealogical account of the nobility of that kingdom*, 9 vols (Edinburgh: David Douglas, 1904–14), V, pp. 27–48.

5 To this day even their field mice remain of Norse origin. See Berry, R., 'The Saga of the Field Mice', *New Scientist*, 13 March 1975), pp. 624–7.

6 Marsden, J., *Somerled and the Emergence of Gaelic Scotland* (East Linton: Tuckwell, 2000), pp. 8–21. See also Boardman, S., 'Lordship in the North-East: The Badenoch Stewarts I, Alexander Stewart, Earl of Buchan, Lord of Badenoch', *Northern Scotland* 16 (1996), pp. 1–29, at p. 6.

7 Marsden, J., 'The Emergence of Somerled', in Marsden, *Somerled*, pp. 23–45, and Paul, 'MacDonald, Lord of the Isles', pp. 28–9. See also Moncreiffe, I., *The Law of Succession* (Edinburgh: John Donald, 2010), pp. 53, 165, 179.

8 Oram, 'The Lordship of the Isles: 1336–1545', p. 128.

9 Gregory, D., *History of the Western Highlands and Isles of Scotland, from A.D. 1493 to A.D. 1625, with a Brief Introductory Sketch, from A.D. 80 to A.D. 1493.* 2nd edition (London: Hamilton, Adams, 1881), pp. 31–2.

10 Paterson, R. C., *The Lords of the Isles: A history of Clan Donald* (Edinburgh: Birlinn, 2001), p. 32. See also Oram, 'The Lordship of the Isles: 1336–1545', p. 130.

11 Paul, 'Macdonald, Lord of the Isles', pp. 37–9.

12 Paul, 'Macdonald, Lord of the Isles', pp. 40–2; Oram, 'The Lordship of the Isles: 1336–1545', p. 131; Mackenzie, A., *History of the Macdonalds and Lords of the Isles* (Inverness: A. & W. Mackenzie, 1881), p. 71.

13 Paterson, *The Lords of the Isles*, p. 32.

14 Mackenzie, *History of the Macdonalds*, p. 61; Oram, 'The Lordship of the Isles: 1336–1545', p. 127; Bannerman, 'The Lordship of the Isles', p. 212; Moncreiffe, *The Law of Succession*, p. 179.

15 Oram, 'The Lordship of the Isles: 1336–1545', p. 127.

16 Bannerman, 'The Lordship of the Isles', p. 216.

17 Boardman, 'Lordship in the North-East', pp. 4–6.

18 Brown, M., 'Fortune's Wheel', in Brown, M., *The Stewart Dynasty in Scotland: James I.* (Edinburgh: Canongate, 1994), pp. 9–39.

19 Boardman, 'Lordship in the North-east', pp. 1–29.

20 Paterson, *The Lords of the Isles*, p. 33.

21 Munro and Munro, *Acts of the Lords of the Isles*, p. lxvi; Bannerman, 'The Lordship of the Isles', p. 214.

22 Oram, 'The Lordship of the Isles: 1336–1545', p. 132.

23 Bannerman, 'The Lordship of the Isles', p. 214.

24 Paterson, *The Lords of the Isles*, p. 38. Also Mackay, W., 'The Battle of Harlaw: Its true place in Scottish history', *Transactions of the Gaelic Society of Inverness* 30 (1922), p. 272.

25 Oram, 'The Lordship of the Isles: 1336–1545', p. 131; Mackenzie, *History of the Macdonalds*, p. 71; Paterson, *The Lords of the Isles*, p. 34

26 Brown, M. 'Regional Lordship in North-East Scotland: The Badenoch Stewarts II, Alexander Stewart Earl of Mar', *Northern Scotland* 16 (1996), pp. 31–53; Mackay, 'The Battle of Harlaw', pp. 269–70.

27 Marsden, J., 'Gall-Gaedhil: Celtic Scotland & the Norse impact', in Marsden, *Somerled*, pp. 1–22, at p. 21.

28 Bannerman, 'The Lordship of the Isles', p. 214; Munro and Munro, *Acts of the Lords of the Isles*, p. lxvi.

29 MacDonald, A. and MacDonald, A., *The Clan Donald*, 3 vols (Inverness: Northern Counties, 1896–1904), I, p. 155.

30 Abercromby, P., *The Martial Atchievements of the Scots Nation*, 2 vols (Edinburgh: Robert Freebairn, 1715), II, p. 239.

31 *Rotuli Scotiae in turri londinensi et in domo capitulari westmonasteriensi asservati. v. 2. Temporibus regum Angliæ Ric. II. Hen. IV. V. VI. Ed. IV. Ric. III. Hen. VII. VIII.* (London: George Eyre and Andrew Strahan, 1813), p. 11a.

32 MacDonald and MacDonald, *The Clan Donald*, I, p. 141.

33 MacBain, A. and Kennedy, J. (eds), 'The Book of Clanranald', in *Reliquiae Celticae: Texts, papers and studies in Gaelic literature and philology left by the late Rev. Alexander Cameron*, 2 vols (Inverness: Northern Counties, 1892), II, pp. 160–3.

34 Emden, A. B., *A Biographical Register of the University of Oxford to A.D. 1500*, 3 vols (Oxford: Clarendon Press, 1958), II, p. 1006.

35 Personal communication, Dr John Noble, Balliol College historian, Oxford.

36 Paul, 'Macdonald, Lord of the Isles', p. 41.

37 Munro and Munro, *Acts of the Lords of the Isles*, p. lxxvi.

38 Brown, M. (1994), 'The Destruction of the Albany Stewarts', in Brown, *The Stewart Dynasty: James I*, pp. 40–71.

39 Macdonald, H., 'History of the Macdonalds', in MacPhail, J. R. N. (ed.), *Highland Papers*, 4 vols (Edinburgh: T. and A. Constable, 1914), I, p. 29.

40 MacDonald and MacDonald, *The Clan Donald*, I, pp. 151–2.

41 Boece [Boethius], *Scotorum Historiae a Prima Gentis Origine* (Paris: Badius Ascensibus, 1527), fol. cccliv, *verso*. See also Buchanan, G., *Rerum Scoticarum Historia* (Edinburgh: Arbuthnet, 1582), Book X, Chapter XVIII, fol. 105.

42 Watt, D. E. R. (ed.), *Walter Bower: Scotichronicon* (Aberdeen: Aberdeen University Press, Edinburgh: Mercat Press, 1987–98), VII, Book XV, pp. 75 –7. Boece, *Scotorum Historiae*, fol. cccliv, verso.

43 Macdonald, 'History of the Macdonalds', p. 29.

44 Boardman, 'Lordship in the North-East', pp. 16–19.

45 Brown, *The Stewart Dynasty: James I*, pp. 37–9.

46 Brown, *The Stewart Dynasty: James I*, p. 32.

47 Simpson, W. D., *The Earldom of Mar* (Aberdeen: Aberdeen University Press, 1949), pp. 44–6.

48 Ditchburn, D., 'Stewart, Alexander, Earl of Mar (c.1380–1435)', *Oxford Dictionary of National Biography* (Oxford: Oxford University Press, 2004; online edition, May 2005 [http://www.oxforddnb.com/view/article/26452, accessed 27 March 2011]. Also Boardman, 'Lordship in the North-East', p. 21.

49 Boardman, 'Lordship in the North-East', p. 34.

50 Watt, *Walter Bower*, p. 75.

51 Forbes, J., 'Memoirs of the House of Forbes' (MSS, Castle Forbes, 1784), pp. 138–9.

52 Ditchburn, D., 'The Pirate, the Policeman and the Pantomime Star: Aberdeen's alternative economy in the early fifteenth century', *Northern Scotland* 12 (1992), pp. 19–34.

3. Early 'Highland' Accounts of the Battle of Harlaw

1 Mackinnon, D., *A Descriptive Catalogue of Gaelic Manuscripts in the Advocates' Library Edinburgh and Elsewhere in Scotland* (Edinburgh: Brown, 1912), p. 325.

2 Munro, J. and Munro, R. W., *Acts of the Lords of the Isles 1336–1493* (Edinburgh: Blackwood, Pillans & Wilson, 1986), pp. lxxix–lxxx.

3 Entry for 1411, in Hennessy, W. M. (ed. and trans.), *The Annals of Loch Cé: A chronicle of Irish affairs from A.D. 1014 to A.D. 1590*, 2 vols (London: Longman, 1871), II, p. 137.

4 Thomson, D. S., 'The Harlaw Brosnachadh: An early fifteenth century curio', in Carney, J. and Greene, D. (eds) *Celtic Studies: Essays in memory of Angus Matheson (1912–1962)* (London: Routledge & Kegan Paul, 1968), pp. 147–89.

5 MacDonald, A. and MacDonald, A., *The MacDonald Collection of Gaelic Poetry* (Inverness: Northern Counties, 1911), p. lxxviii.

6 McLeod, W. and Bateman, M., *Duanaire na Sracaire: Songbook of the Pillagers: Anthology of Scotland's Gaelic verse to 1600* (Edinburgh: Birlinn, 2007), pp. 229–33; Thomson, 'The Harlaw Brosnachadh', p.166.

7 University of Glasgow Library, MS Gen 1042/222a, and MS Gen 1042/97. Thomson, 'The Harlaw Brosnachadh', p.166, also refers to a 'modernised' version, 'undertaken by some industrious gentleman with a perverse interest in lexicography', which he dates between 1780 and 1804.

8 Macgregor, M., 'The Genealogical Histories of Gaelic Scotland', in Woolf, D and Fox, A. (eds), *The Spoken Word: Oral culture in the British Isles, 1500–1800* (Manchester: Manchester University Press, 2002), pp. 196–239, at p. 197.

9 Thomson, 'The Harlaw Brosnachadh', p. 150.

10 Simpson, W. D., *The Earldom of Mar* (Aberdeen: Aberdeen University Press, 1949), p. 52.

11 Meek, D. E., 'The World of William Livingston', in McClure, J. D., Kirk, J. M. and Storrie, M. (eds), *A Land that Lies Westward: Language and culture in Islay and Argyll* (Edinburgh: John Donald, 2009), pp. 149–72. Or indeed of a totally imaginary battle such as recounted in Meek, D. E., '"Norsemen and noble stewards": The MacSween poem in the Book of the Dean of Lismore', *Cambrian Medieval Celtic Studies* 34 (1997), pp. 1–49.

12 Haddow, A. J., *The History and Structure of Ceol Mor* (n.p., 1892), p. 96. See also Purser, J., *Scotland's Music* (Edinburgh and London: Mainstream, 2007), p. 86.

13 'Observations of Mr. Dioness Campbell, Deane of Limerick, on the West Isles of Scotland. A.D. 1596', in *Miscellany of the Maitland Club: Consisting of original papers and other documents illustrative of the history and literature of Scotland*, 4 vols (Glasgow: W. Eadie and Co., 1833–1847), IV, Part 1, pp. 35–59.

14 Scott, W., *Tales of a Grandfather*, 3 vols (Edinburgh: Cadell & Co; London: Simpkin & Marshall; Dublin: John Cumming, 1828), II, p. 85.

15 Watt, D.E.R. (ed.), *Scotichronicon by Walter Bower*, 9 vols (Aberdeen: Aberdeen University Press, and Edinburgh: Mercat Press, 1987–98).

16 'The Book of Cupar' or the 'Coupar Angus MS' (National Library of Scotland, Adv. MS 35.1.7).

17 Bower. W., *Scotichronicon*, Book XV, Chapter 21, in the Cambridge Corpus

Christi College MS 171, a fair copy originally belonging to Inchcolm Abbey, written in the mid 1440s and then amended under Bower's supervision until his death in 1449; Watt, *Scotichronicon*, VIII, Preface, pp. ix–xi., pp. xvi–xx. The translation follows that of Donald Watt with a major alteration: '*nongenti*' is rendered as 'nine hundred' rather than 'ninety'; Watt, *Scotichronicon*, VIII, pp. 75, 77.

18 Watt, *Scotichronicon*, XV, Chapter 21. Watt also notes that 'Bower apparently cannot list the gentlemen of Buchan . . . in the same detail as he has done for those from Angus and Mearns'. Watt, *Scotichronicon*, VIII, p. 184.

19 Goodall, W., *Joannis de Fordun Scotichronicon, cum Supplementis ac Continuatione Walteri Boweri*, 2 vols (Edinburgh: 1759), II, p. 445, which is based mainly on Edinburgh University Library MS 186, also contains this amendment.

20 Skene, F. J. H. (ed. and trans.), *Liber Pluscardensis*, 2 vols (Edinburgh: W. Paterson, 1877–80).

21 Skene, *Liber Pluscardensis*, Book I, ix–xvii, xxiii.

22 Skene, *Liber Pluscardensis*, Book X, Chapter xxii.

23 Mair [Major], J., *Historia Maioris Britanniae, tam Angli[a]e q[uam] Scoti[a]e, per Ioanne[m] Maiorem, nomine quidem Scotum, professione autem theologum, e veterum monumentis concinnata* (Paris, 1521).

24 Broadie, A., 'John Mair (c.1467–1550)', in Matthew, H. C. G. and Harrison, B. (eds), *Oxford Dictionary of National Biography* (Oxford: Oxford University Press, 2004; online edition, May 2011).

25 Constable, A. D. (ed. and trans.), *A History of Greater Britain, as well England as Scotland compiled from the ancient authorities by John Major, by name indeed a Scot, but by profession a theologian, 1521, edited and translated by Constable, A. D.* (Edinburgh: T. & A. Constable,1892), *Book* VI, Chapter X, pp. 348–9.

26 Boece [Boethius], H., *Scotorum Historiae a Prima Gentis Origine* (Paris: Badius Ascensibus, 1527 [British Library gives date of 1526]).

27 Royan, N., 'Hector Boece (c.1465–1536)', in Matthew, H. C. G. and Harrison, B. (eds.), *Oxford Dictionary of National Biography* (Oxford: Oxford University Press, 2004; online edition, 2008).

28 Boece, *Scotorum Historiae*, fol. ccliv, verso. English version based on translations by Patrick Edwards and Robin Nisbet.

29 Buchanan, G., *Rerum Scoticarum Historia* (Edinburgh: Alexander Arbuthnet, 1582).

30 Abbott, D. M., 'George Buchanan (1506–1582)', in Matthew, H. C. G. and Harrison, B., (eds.), *Oxford Dictionary of National Biography* (Oxford University Press, 2004; online edition, 2006).

31 Buchanan, *Rerum Scoticarum Historia*, Book X, Chapter XVIII. Based on a translation by Patrick Edwards. (A variable English translation was given by Boyle, J., *George Buchanan's History of Scotland in Twenty Books* (Aberdeen, 1771), X, p. 373. Boyle, for example, mistranslates '*decem millibus*' in Donald's army as only '1000'.)

4. The 'Ramsay ballad': 'The Battle of Harlaw'

1 Ramsay, A., *Ever Green, being a Collection of Scots Poems, wrote by the Ingenious before 1600*, 2 vols (Edinburgh: Ruddiman, 1724), I, pp. 78–90.

2 Brown, M. E., *The Bedesman and the Hodbearer: The epistolary friendship of Francis James Child* [1825–1896] *and William Walker* [1840–1931] (Aberdeen: University of Aberdeen, 2001), p. 24.

3 Walker, W. (ed.), *Letters on Scottish Ballads from Professor Francis J. Child to W. W.* [William Walker] (Aberdeen: Bon-Accord Press, 1930), p. 4.

4 Rieuwerts, S., 'The Historical Moorings of "The Gipsy laddie"; Johnny Faa and Lady Cassilis', in Harris, J., ed., *The Ballad and Oral Literature* (Cambridge, Massachusetts: Harvard University Press, 1991), pp. 78–96; Olson, I. A., 'The Dreadful Death of the Bonny Earl of Moray: Clues from the Carpenter Song Collection', *Folk Music Journal* 7 (1997), pp. 281–310.

5 Olson, I. A., 'The Bonny Lass o' Fyvie or Pretty Peggy of Derby?', *Review of Scottish Culture* 22 (2010), pp. 150–63.

6 Child, F. J. (ed.), *The English and Scottish Popular Ballads*, 5 vols (Boston: Houghton Mifflin, 1882–98), III, p. 317 [Child No. 163].

7 Greig, G., 'The Battle of Harlaw: Folk-Song of the North-East XI', *Buchan Observer*, 11 February 1908; Shuldham-Shaw, P., *et al.* (eds), *The Greig–Duncan Folk Song Collection*, 8 vols (Aberdeen: Aberdeen University Press and Edinburgh: Mercat Press, 1981–2002), I, p. 527 [re. 'The Battle of Harlaw', song no. 112].

8 Bronson, B. H., 'The Battle of Harlaw: Child 163', in *The Traditional Tunes of the Child Ballads*, 4 vols (Princeton: Princeton University Press, 1959–72), III, pp. 117–25. He makes a very tentative suggestion for another tune, 'Pitt your Shirt on Monday', but using its opening phrases, Andrew Hunter indeed movingly sang the 'Ramsay ballad' to it on Bonnie Rideout's *Harlaw*, a double CD from Tulloch Music Ltd. tm525, Alexandria USA, I, track 6.

9 Shuldham Shaw *et al.*, *The Greig–Duncan Folk Song Collection*, I, p.527; Clyne, N., *Ballads from Scottish History* (Edinburgh: Edmonston & Douglas, 1863), p. 244.

10 Laing, D., *Early Metrical Tales* (Edinburgh, 1826), pp. 228–39.

11 Aytoun, W. E. (ed.), *The Ballads of Scotland*, 2 vols (Edinburgh: Blackwood, 1858), I, p. 65.

12 Simpson, W. D., *The Earldom of Mar* (Aberdeen: Aberdeen University Press, 1949), pp. 49–50.

13 Alexander, W. McC., *Place Names of Aberdeenshire* (Aberdeen: Spalding Club, 1952), p. 285.

14 Mackay, W., 'The Battle of Harlaw: Its True Place in Scottish History', *Transactions of the Gaelic Society of Inverness* 30 (1922), pp. 267–85, at p. 284.

15 Clyne, *Ballads from Scottish History*, pp. 247–8.

16 Simpson, *The Earldom of Mar*, pp. 52–3. Mar's eternal gratitude for the role Forbes played in the success of the battle is recorded in Forbes, J., 'Memoirs of the House of Forbes'. This manuscript in Castle Forbes is dated 1784.

17 Clyne, *Ballads from Scottish History*, pp. 244–7; Shuldham Shaw *et al.*, *The Greig–Duncan Folk Song Collection*, I, song 112, p. 527.

18 Royan, N., 'John Bellenden', in Matthew, H. C. G. and Harrison, B. (eds) *Oxford Dictionary of National Biography* (Oxford: Oxford University Press, 2004; online edition, 2006). See also Royan, N., 'Hector Boece', in Matthew, H. C. G. and Harrison, B. (eds), *Oxford Dictionary of National Biography* (Oxford: Oxford University Press, 2004; online edition, 2006).

19 Maitland, T. (ed.), *The History and Chronicles of Scotland: Written in Latin by Hector Boece, Canon of Aberdeen, and Translated by John Bellenden, Archdeacon of Moray and Canon of Ross*, 2 vols (Edinburgh: W. and C. Tait, 1821), II, pp. 485–6. This edition is based on the printed version of c.1536. Variants in the earlier manuscript presented to King James V are given within square brackets. For this earlier version, see Chambers, R. W., Batho, E. C. and Husbands, H. W. (eds), *The Chronicles of Scotland Compiled by Hector Boece. Translated into Scots by John Bellenden 1531*, 2 vols (Edinburgh and London: Blackwood, 1938–41), II, pp. 370–1.

20 Simpson, *The Earldom of Mar*, p. 50, although he gave no evidence for this statement.

21 Thomas, A., 'James V (1512–1542)', in Mathew and Harrison, *Oxford Dictionary of National Biography*.

22 Stewart, W., 'The Buik of the Croniclis of Scotland', W. B. Turnbull (ed.), 3 vols (Rolls Series, 6) (London, 1858), pp. 495–7. See also Pollard, A. F., 'Stewart, William (fl. 1499–1541)' (revised by McGinley, J. K.), in Mathew and Harrison, *Oxford Dictionary of National Biography*.

23 Wedderburn, R., *The Complaynt of Scotland (c. 1550)* (Edinburgh: Scottish Text Society, 1979), pp. 50–1.

5. The Seventeenth and Early Eighteenth-century Accounts

1 Macdonald, H., 'History of the Macdonalds', in Macphail, J. R. N. (ed.), *Highland Papers*, 3 vols (Edinburgh: T. and A. Constable, 1914–34), I, p. 10.

2 Macgregor, M., 'The Genealogical Histories of Gaelic Scotland', in Woolf, D. and Fox, A. (eds), *The Spoken Word: Oral culture in the British Isles, 1500–1800* (Manchester and New York: Manchester University Press, 2002), pp. 196–239, at p. 197.

3 Logan, J. and Alexander, S., *The Scottish Gael*, 2 vols (Inverness: Mackenzie, 1876), I, p. 155.

4 Davidson, J., *Inverurie and the Earldom of the Garioch* (Edinburgh: David Douglas and Aberdeen: A. Brown and Co., 1878), pp. 83–98, at p. 94.

5 MacBain, A., and Kennedy, J. (eds), 'The Book of Clanranald', in *Reliquiae Celticae: Texts papers and studies in Gaelic literature and philology left by the late Rev. Alexander Cameron*, 2 vols (Inverness: Northern Counties, 1894), II, pp. 137–47, 149–288.

6 Davidson, A. M. [1887–1935], 'The Red Book of Clanranald', *Scottish Notes and Queries*, 3rd Series (March 1934), 12, pp. 43–5.

7 'Gavin Greig: Correspondence from various Gaelic scholars to Miss A. M. Davidson, concerning the 'Leabhar Dearg' of Clan Ranald 1934–1937'(Aberdeen University Library, MS 3017/7/9). The title is misleading; the correspondence

belonged to Alexander Keith, then editor of the *Aberdeen Daily Journal*. Miss Davidson was an Aberdeen resident.

8 MacBain and Kennedy, 'The Book of Clanranald', pp. 160–3.

9 'The Black Book of Clanranald' (National Museums of Scotland, MCR 40), f61r.

10 'The Red Book of Clanranald' (National Museums of Scotland, MCR39), pp. 40–1.

11 Dineen, P. S., *Foclóir Gaedhilge agus Béarla: An Irish–English dictionary* (Dublin: Irish Texts Society, revised 1927; online reprint, 1979).

12 Thomson, D. S., 'The Harlaw Brosnachadh: An early fifteenth century curio. In *Celtic Studies: Essays in memory of Angus Matheson (1912–1962)* (London: Routledge & Kegan Paul, 1968), pp. 147–89.

13 Thomson, 'The Harlaw Brosnachadh', p. 150.

14 Toit, A. D., 'Abercromby, Patrick (*b.* 1656, *d.* in or after 1716)', in Matthew, H. C. G. and Harrison, B. (eds), *Oxford Dictionary of National Biography*, (Oxford: Oxford University Press, 2004; online edition, 2006).

15 Abercromby. P., *Martial Atchievements* [sic] *of the Scots* Nation, 2 vols (Edinburgh: Freebairn, 1711 and 1715), II, p. 239.

16 Irvine, J. [8th of Kingcausie, 1664–1740], 'The privat History of the Irvins of Kingcausie since the tyme they descended from the Honorable familie of Drum Irvine', Kingcausie House. It appears in two manuscript versions, dated c.1720 and c.1732. Earlier papers, including those of John, 7th of Kingcausie, appear to have been destroyed when the house was burnt around 1680. Personal communication from James Irvine-Fortescue in letter of 13 January 2001.

17 Kelly, J. N. D., *The Oxford Dictionary of the Popes* (Oxford: Oxford University Press, 1986), pp. 236–9.

18 In Clark, J. S. (ed.), *Genealogical Collections concerning Families in Scotland, made by Walter Macfarlane. 1750–1751*, 2 vols (Edinburgh: T. and A. Constable for Scottish History Society, 1900), I, pp. 125–6. This appears to be based on 'A genealogical account of the family of Maclean from its first settling in the Island of Mull and parts adjacent about the year 1390 to the year 1716. – Written at the desire of the Laird of MacFarlane in the year 1734 by Hector Macleane younger of Gruline in the Isle of Mull Shire of Argyle' (NLS Acc 7609). The National Library of Scotland states that this has certainly a close relationship to the copy found in the papers of Walter Macfarlane the antiquary, at shelf mark Adv.MS.35.4.8(i), pp. 175 ff. Clark's text seems to be based on that written by Hector Maclean, although some rearranging was done.

6. The Later Eighteenth-century Accounts: Lord Forbes and his Ballad

1 [Forbes, A. of Brux], *Don: A poem* (Edinburgh: Mair, 1814), pp. 36–47.

2 Walker, W., *The Bards of Bon-Accord 1375–1860* (Aberdeen: Edmund and Spark, 1887), pp. 166–75.

3 Moncreiffe, I. and Hicks, D., *The Highland Clans* (London: Barrie & Rockcliffe, 1967), p. 88.

4 Tayler A. and Tayler, H. (eds), *The House of Forbes* (Aberdeen: Third Spalding Club, 1937), pp. 25, 27.

5 Davidson, W., 'The Battle of Harlaw', in *Bon-Accord: Coronation and Harlaw Number* (Aberdeen, 1878), p. 1.

6 Forbes, J., 'Memoirs of the House of Forbes' (MSS Castle Forbes, 1784), pp. 136–9.

7 Tayler and Tayler, *The House of Forbes*, p. 3.

8 Child, F. J. (ed.), *The English and Scottish Popular Ballads*, 5 vols (Boston: Houghton Mifflin, 1882–98), III, p. 317 [Child No. 163].

9 Laing, A., *The Thistle of Scotland* (Aberdeen: J. Booth Jun. 1823), p. 92.

10 Buchan, D., 'History and Harlaw', in Lyle, E. B. (ed.), *Ballad Studies* (Cambridge, 1976), pp. 29–40, at p. 38. Printed previously in *Journal of the Folklore Institute* 5 (1968), pp. 58–67. Republished in Nicolaisen, W. and Moreira, J. (eds.), *The Ballad and the Folklorist: The Collected Papers of David Buchan* (St. John's, Newfoundland, Memorial University Press, 2014), pp. 14-23.

11 Shuldham-Shaw, P., *et al.* (eds), *The Greig–Duncan Folk Song Collection*, 8 vols (Aberdeen: Aberdeen University Press, and Edinburgh: Mercat Press 1981–2002), I, song 112, pp. 302–13.

12 Shuldham Shaw *et al.*, *The Greig–Duncan Folk Song Collection*, I, p. 527; Greig, G, 'The Battle of Harlaw: Folk-song of the North-East XI', *Buchan Observer*, 11 February 1908.

13 Buchan, 'History and Harlaw', pp. 35–6.

14 Olson, I. A. and Morris, J., 'Mussel-Mou'd Charlie's (Charles Leslie) 1745 Song: "McLeod's Defeat at Inverury" ', *Aberdeen University Review* 58 (Autumn 2000), pp. 317–31. See also Tayler, A. and Tayler, H., *Jacobites of Aberdeenshire and Banffshire in the Forty-Five*, 2nd edition (Aberdeen: Milne & Hutchison, 1928), pp. 40–4.

15 A feature which marks not just this verse but the whole ballad – it is sung in Scots. As Hamish Henderson would remark, the 'known historical' ballads were usually sung in a curiously 'high' form. See also Cowan, E., *The People's Past* (Edinburgh: Edinburgh University Student Publication Board, 1980), pp. 105–6.

16 Forbes, 'Memoirs', pp. 138–9. Also Simpson, W. D., *The Earldom of Mar* (Aberdeen: Aberdeen University Press, 1949), p. 49.

17 Greig, G., 'Sir James the Rose: A historical ballad', *Buchan Observer*, 25 August 1908.

18 Shuldham Shaw *et al.*, *The Greig–Duncan Folk Song Collection*, II, song 235, version A, pp. 178–88.

19 Moncreiffe, I. and Hicks, D., *The Highland Clans* (London: Barrie & Rockcliffe, 1967), pp. 60–1.

20 Moncreiffe and Hicks, *The Highland Clans*, p. 60.

21 Shuldham Shaw *et al.*, *The Greig–Duncan Folk Song Collection*, II, song 112, version D, pp. 306–7.

22 Buchan, 'History and Harlaw', pp. 34–5.

23 Donaldson, W., 'Bonny Highland Laddie: The making of a myth', *Scottish Literary Journal* 3:2 (1976), pp. 30–50. See also Olson, I. A., 'Contemporary

Scottish Music and Song: An introduction', in Zenzinger, P. (ed.), *Scotland: Literature, Culture, Politics* (Heidelberg: Carl Winter, 1989), pp. 139–66.

24 Abercromby. P., *Martial Atchievements* [sic] *of the Scots Nation* (Edinburgh: Freebairn, 1715), pp. 212–13. Paul, J. B. (ed.), *The Scots Peerage: Founded on Wood's edition of Sir Robert Douglas's peerage of Scotland: containing an historical and genealogical account of the nobility of that kingdom*, 9 vols (Edinburgh: David Douglas, 1904–14), V, p. 41; Mackay, W., 'The Battle of Harlaw: Its true place in Scottish history', *Transactions of the Gaelic Society of Inverness* 30 (1922), pp. 267–85, at p. 282. Mackay's claim that Donald actually attended Oxford is unfounded, although he was indeed offered a safe transit to attend there for six years by the young Richard II (see Chapter 2).

25 Simpson, *The Earldom of Mar*, p. 49.

26 Hill, J. M., *Celtic Warfare* (Edinburgh: John Donald, 1995), pp. 1, 9–16.

27 Simpson, *The Earldom of Mar*, p. 46.

28 Simpson, *The Earldom of Mar*, pp. 52–3.

29 Simpson, *The Earldom of Mar*, p. 56.

30 Tayler and Tayler, *The House of Forbes*, p. 31.

31 Tayler and Tayler, *The House of Forbes*, p. 37; Slade, H. G., 'Druminnor, Formerly Castle Forbes', *Proceedings of the Society of Antiquaries of Scotland* 99 (1996/7), pp. 148–66.

32 Paul, *The Scots Peerage*, V, p. 42.

33 Simpson, *The Earldom of Mar*, p. 57.

34 Simpson, *The Earldom of Mar*, p. 52.

35 Buchan, 'History and Harlaw', p. 38.

36 Buchan, 'History and Harlaw', pp. 35–7; Henderson, H., 'Ballad Studies', *Tocher* 27 (1977), p. 186.

37 Brown, M. E., *Child's Unfinished Masterpiece* (Urbana, Chicago and Springfield: Illinois Press, 2011), pp. 124–5.

38 Keith, A. (ed.), *Last Leaves of Traditional Ballads and Ballad Airs* (Aberdeen: The Buchan Club, 1925), p. 102.

39 Bronson, B. H., 'The Battle of Harlaw. Child No 163', in *The Traditional Tunes of the Child Ballads*, 4 vols (Princeton, New Jersey: Princeton University Press, 1966), III, pp. 117–25.

40 Dalrymple, C. E. to Child, F. J., 6 April 1888 (Houghton Library, Harvard University, bMS Am 2349, vol 26).

41 Buchan, 'History and Harlaw', pp. 32–3 and endnote 4.

42 Moncreiffe and Hicks, *The Highland Clans*, p. 178.

43 Brown, M. 'Regional Lordship in North-East Scotland: The Badenoch Stewarts II, Alexander Stewart Earl of Mar', *Northern Scotland* 16 (1996), pp. 34–7.

7. The Early Nineteenth-century Accounts

1 Scott, W. (1771–1832), *The Antiquary*, 3 vols (Edinburgh: 1816), III, pp. 72, 221–4, and note 10.

2 Paul, J. B. (ed.), *The Scots Peerage: Founded on Wood's edition of Sir Robert Douglas's peerage of Scotland: containing an historical and genealogical account of the nobility of that kingdom*, 9 vols (Edinburgh: David Douglas, 1904–14), V, pp. 586–9.

3 Boardman, S., 'Lordship in the North-East: The Badenoch Stewarts I, Alexander Stewart, Earl of Buchan, Lord of Badenoch', *Northern Scotland* 16 (1996), pp. 1–29; Brown, M., 'Regional Lordship in North-East Scotland: The Badenoch Stewarts, II', *Northern Scotland* 16, (1996), pp. 31–53; Ditchburn, D., 'Stewart, Alexander, Earl of Mar (*c.*1380–1435)', *Oxford Dictionary of National Biography* (Oxford University Press, 2004; online edition 2005).

4 Watt, D. E. R. (ed), *Scotichronicon by Walter Bower*, 9 vols (Aberdeen: Aberdeen University Press, Edinburgh: Mercat Press 1987–98), VIII, Book XV, p. 293.

5 Jackson, R. N., 'The Noble Anglo-Saxons?', *Aberdeen University Review* 57 (Spring 1998), pp. 207–19.

6 Marsden, J., 'Gall-Gaedhail. Celtic Scotland & the Norse Impact', in *Somerled and the Emergence of Gaelic Scotland* (East Linton: Tuckwell, 2000), pp. 1–22.

7 Laing, A. [1778–1838], *The Caledonian Itinerary*, 2 vols (Aberdeen: Laing, 1819), I, p. 155.

8 Laing, D., *Early Metrical Tales* (Edinburgh: W. & D. Laing; London: J. Duncan, 1826), pp. xlv, 229–39.

9 Scott, W., *Tales of a Grandfather*, 3 vols (Edinburgh: Cadell & Co; London, Simpkin & Marshall; Dublin: John Cumming, 1828), II, Chapter XVIII, p. 85.

10 Tytler, P. F., *History of Scotland*, 9 vols (Edinburgh: W. Tait, 1828-42), III, pp. 170–8.

11 Fry, M., 'Tytler, Patrick Fraser (1791–1849)', in Matthew, H. C. G. and Harrison, B. (eds), *Oxford Dictionary of National Biography* (Oxford: Oxford University Press, 2004; online edition, 2013).

12 By a Seneachie, *An Historical and Genealogical Account of the Clan MacLean from its First Settlement at Castle Duart, in the Isle of Mull, to the Present Period* (London: Smith, Elder and Co. Cornhill; Edinburgh: Laing and Forbes, 1838), pp. 10–14. The 'Seneachie' has not been identified, although an edition published in Cincinnati in 1889 by Robert Clarke & Co., stated the author was a 'J. P. MacLean'.

13 In Clark, J. T. (ed.), *Genealogical Collections Concerning Families in Scotland, made by Walter Macfarlane. 1750–1751*, 2 vols (Edinburgh: T. and A. Constable for Scottish History Society, 1900), I, pp. 125–6. Although the account has the asterisked footnote 'James Major [History of Scotland], lib. vi. anno 1411', this does not in fact refer to any sword exchange. See also *Miscellanea Scotica: A collection of tracts relating to the history, antiquities, topography, and literature of Scotland*, 4 vols (Glasgow: Wylie, 1818–20), II, p. 70.

8. The Later Nineteenth-century Accounts

1　Simson, H. [1788–1850], 'Parish of the Chapel of Garioch', in 'The Parish of Aberdeen', in *The New Statistical Account of Scotland*, 15 vols (Edinburgh: William Blackwood & Sons, 1845), XII, pp. 566–70.

2　Simpson, W. D., *The Earldom of Mar* (Aberdeen: Aberdeen University Press, 1949), p. 53, note 42.

3　Personal communication from the late Jack Philip, farmer, of Mill of Lumphart, by Old Meldrum.

4　Irvine, J. [8th of Kingcausie, 1664–1740], 'The privat History of the Irvins of Kingcausie since the tyme they descended from the Honorable familie of Drum Irvine' (Kingcausie House. Manuscript version dated c.1720).

5　Clyne, N., 'The Burghers of Bon-Accord', in *Ballads from Scottish History* (Edinburgh: Edmonston and Douglas, 1863), pp. 126–249.

6　Henderson, J. A. (ed.), 'Norval Clyne', in *The Society of Advocates in Aberdeen: List of Members*, Aberdeen University Studies No. 60 (Aberdeen: Aberdeen University, 1912), pp. 126–7. Also 'Norval Clyne', Obituary, *Aberdeen Journal*, 2 January 1888.

7　Hill Burton, J., *History of Scotland*, 7 vols (Edinburgh: William Blackwood, 1809–81), III, pp. 99–102.

8　Fry, M., 'Burton, John Hill (1809–1881)', in Matthew, H. C. G. and Harrison, B. (eds), in *Oxford Dictionary of National Biography* (Oxford: Oxford University Press, 2004; online edition, 2004).

9　Davidson, J., 'The Battle of Harlaw and its Times', in *Inverurie and the Earldom of the Garioch* (Edinburgh: David Douglas; Aberdeen: A. Brown and Co., 1878), pp. 83–98.

10　Johnston, W. (ed.), 'John Davidson', in *Roll of the Graduates of the University of Aberdeen (1860–1900)* (Aberdeen: Aberdeen University Press, 1906), p. 124.

11　Simpson, *The Earldom of Mar*, p. 53.

12　Irvine-Fortescue, J. A., Personal communication, letter of 30 January 2001.

13　Mackenzie, A., *History of the Macdonalds and Lords of the Isles* (Inverness: A. & W. Mackenzie, 1881).

14　MacGregor, M., 'The Genealogical Histories of Gaelic Scotland', in Fox, A. and Woolf, D. (eds), *The Spoken Word: Oral culture in Britain 1500–1850* (Manchester and New York: Manchester University Press, 2002), pp. 196–239, at p. 200.

15　Gregory, D., *History of the Western Highlands and Isles of Scotland, from A.D. 1493 to A.D. 1625, with a Brief Introductory Sketch, from A.D. 80 to A.D. 1493*, 2nd edition (London: Hamilton, Adams, 1881), pp. 31–2.

16　Skene, W. F., *The Highlanders of Scotland*, 2 vols (London: John Murray, 1837), II, pp. 71–3.

17　Mackay, A. J. G., 'Skene, William Forbes (1809–1892)', Rev. Sellar, W. D. H., in Matthew, H. C. G. and Harrison, B. (eds), *Oxford Dictionary of National Biography* (Oxford: Oxford University Press, 2004; online edition, 2006).

18　MacDonald, A. and MacDonald, A., 'Donald of Harlaw', in *The Clan Donald*, 3 vols (Inverness: Northern Counties, 1896), I, pp. 130–68.

9. Harlaw Legends and Myths

1 Wimberley, D., *A Short Account of the Family of Irvine of Drum in the County of Aberdeen* (Inverness: Northern Chronicle, 1893), pp. 2–3.
2 Forbes Leslie, J., *The Irvines of Drum and Collateral Branches* (Aberdeen, 1909), pp. 32–8.
3 Davidson, J., *Inverurie and the Earldom of the Garioch* (Edinburgh: David Douglas and Aberdeen, A. Brown and Co., 1878), pp. 83-98; Wimberley, *A Short Account of the Family of Irvine of Drum*, p. 3.
4 Irvine-Fortescue, J. A., 'A Few Truths on Gude Sir Alexander: Who was the Harlaw hero?', *Deeside Field* (1988), pp. 40–3.
5 Irvine-Fortescue, J. A., personal communication, letter, 17 January 2001.
6 Mackintosh, D. M., *The Irvines of Drum and their Cadet Lines 1300–1750* (Greenville, South Carolina: Southern Historical Press, 1998), p. 36.
7 See the perceptive essays by Martin MacGregor, Dauvit Brown and Stephen Boardman, in Broun, D. and MacGregor, M. (eds), *Mìorun Mòr Nan Gall, 'The Great Ill-Will of the Lowlander'? Lowland perceptions of the Highlands,medieval and modern* (Chippenham and Eastbourne: Anthony Rowe, 2009), pp. 7–48.

10. Retreat and Abasement?

1 Cody, E.G. and Murison, W. (eds), *The Historie of Scotland written first in Latin by the most reverend and worthy Jhone Leslie,*[1527–1596] *Bishop of Ross, and translated in Scottish by Father James Dalrymple* [fl. 1596], *Seuint Buke* (Scottish Text Society: Edinburgh, 1888-95), Seventh Book, p.33.
2 Paul, J. B. (ed.), *The Scots Peerage: Founded on Wood's edition of Sir Robert Douglas's peerage of Scotland: containing an historical and genealogical account of the nobility of that kingdom,* 9 vols (Edinburgh: David Douglas, 1904–14), VII, p. 42.
3 Macdonald, H., 'History of the Macdonalds', in Macphail, J. R. N. (ed.), *Highland Papers,* 4 vols (Edinburgh: T. and A. Constable, 1914), I, p. 32.
4 Mackenzie, A., *History of the Macdonalds and Lords of the Isles* (Inverness: A. & W. Mackenzie, 1881), p. 65.
5 Macdonald, 'History of the Macdonalds', pp. 33–4.
6 MacDonald, A. and MacDonald, A., 'Donald of Harlaw', in MacDonald, A. and MacDonald, A., *The Clan Donald,* 3 vols (Inverness: Northern Counties, 1896), I, p.165.
7 Watt, D. E. R. (ed.), *Scotichronicon by Walter Bower,* 9 vols (Aberdeen: Aberdeen University Press, Edinburgh: Mercat Press, 1987–98), VII, Book XV, pp. 76–7.
8 MacDonald and MacDonald, *The Clan Donald,* I, pp. 165-7.
9 Thomson, T. (ed.), *The Accounts of the Great Chamberlains of Scotland; and some other officers of the crown, rendered at the Exchequer. Scotland. (1768–1852),* 4 vols (Edinburgh: Bannatyne Club, 1817–36), III, pp. 47, 66.
10 Stuart, J. *et al.* (eds), *The Exchequer Rolls of Scotland = Rotuli scaccarii regum Scotorum Scotland. Court of Exchequer,* 23 vols (Edinburgh: General Register House, 1878–1908), IV, p. 239.

11 Boece [Boethius], *Scotorum Historiae a Prima Gentis Origine* (Paris: Badius Ascensibus, 1527), fol. ccliv, verso.

12 Chambers, R. W., Batho, E. C. and Husbands, H. W. (eds), *The Chronicles of Scotland compiled by Hector Boece. Translated into Scots by John Bellenden 1531*, 2 vols (Edinburgh and London: W. Blackwood & Sons, 1938–41.), II, pp. 370–1.

13 Abercromby, P., *Martial Atchievements* [sic] *of the Scots Nation*, 2 vols (Edinburgh: Freebairn, 1711 and 1715), II, pp. 237–9.

14 Mackenzie, A., *History of the Macdonalds and Lords of the Isles* (Inverness: A. & W. Mackenzie, 1881), p. 65.

15 MacDonald and MacDonald, *The Clan Donald*, I, p. 165.

16 Mackenzie, *History of the Macdonalds*, p. 65.

17 Watt, *Scotichronicon*, VIII, pp. 76–7.

18 Cody and Murison, *The Historie of Scotland*, p. 33.

19 Forbes, J., 'Memoirs of the House of Forbes' (MSS Castle Forbes, 1784), p. 139.

20 MacDonald and MacDonald, *The Clan Donald*, pp. 166–7.

21 Campbell, M. and Sandeman, M., 'Mid Argyll: An archaeological survey', *Proceedings of the Society of Antiquaries of Scotland* (1961/2), xcv, p. 94.

22 MacBain, M. A. and Kennedy, J. (eds), *Reliquiae Celticae: Texts, papers and studies in Gaelic literature and philology left by the late Rev. Alexander Cameron, LL.D* [1827–1888], 2 vols (Inverness: Northern Counties, 1892–4), II, pp. 160–3. For this fresh translation of the *Books of Clanranald* by Ronald Black and Colm Ó Baoill, see Chapter 6.

23 Boardman, S., 'Lordship in the North-East: The Badenoch Stewarts I, Alexander Stewart, Earl of Buchan, Lord of Badenoch', *Northern Scotland* 16 (1996), pp. 20–3.

24 Simpson, W. D., 'The Break-up of the Earldom', in Simpson, W. D., *The Earldom of Mar* (Aberdeen: Aberdeen University Press, 1949), pp. 62–3.

25 Paul, *The Scots Peerage*, VII, pp. 242–3.

26 Brown, M., 'The Destruction of the Albany Stewarts', in Brown, M., *The Stewart Dynasty in Scotland: James I* (Edinburgh: Canongate, 1994), p. 103. Also Watt, *Scotichronicon*, XVI, Chapter 16, pp. 28–36.

27 Paul, *The Scots Peerage*, V, p. 46.

11. Conclusions

1 Macdonald, H., 'History of the Macdonalds' ['*The Sleat History*'], in Macphail, J. R. N. (ed.), *Highland Papers*, 4 vols (Edinburgh: T. and A. Constable, 1914), I, p. 10.

2 Brown, M., *The Stewart Dynasty in Scotland: James I* (Edinburgh: Canongate, 1994), p. 26.

3 Mackay, W., 'The Battle of Harlaw: Its true place in Scottish history', *Transactions of the Gaelic Society of Inverness* 30 (1922), pp. 267–85.

4 'William Mackay', Obituary, *Aberdeen University Review* 15 (1927–8), p. 286.

5 Brown, *The Stewart Dynasty: James I*, p. 102.

6 Gregory, D., *History of the Western Highlands and Isles of Scotland, from A.D. 1493 to A.D. 1625, with a brief introductory sketch, from A.D. 80 to A.D. 1493*, 2nd edition (London: Hamilton, Adams, 1881), pp. 31–2.

7 MacGregor, M., 'The Genealogical Histories of Gaelic Scotland', in Fox, A. and Woolf, D. (eds), *The Spoken Word: Oral culture in Britain 1500–1850* (Manchester and New York: Manchester University Press, 2002), pp. 196–239, at p. 199.

8 MacGregor, 'The Genealogical Histories of Gaelic Scotland', pp. 196–239.

9 MacGregor, M, 'Gaelic Barbarity and Scottish Identity in the Later Middle Ages', in Broun, D. and MacGregor, M. (eds), *Mìorun Mòr Nan Gall: 'The Great Ill-Will of the Lowlander'? Lowland perceptions of the Highlands, medieval and modern* (Chippenham and Eastbourne: Anthony Rowe, 2009), pp. 7–48, at pp. 47–8.

10 Moncreiffe, I. and Hicks, D., *The Highland Clans* (London: Barrie & Rockcliffe, 1967), p. 178.

11 Boardman, 'The Gaelic World and the Early Stewart Court', pp. 83–109, at pp. 108–9.

12 'Observations of Mr. Dioness Campbell, Deane of Limerick, on the West Isles of Scotland. A.D. 1596', in *Miscellany of the Maitland Club: Consisting of original papers and other documents illustrative of the history and literature of Scotland*, 4 vols (Glasgow: W. Eadie and Co., 1833–47), IV, Part 1, pp. 35–59.

13 MacDonald, A. and MacDonald, A., 'Donald of Harlaw', in *The Clan Donald*, 3 vols (Inverness: Northern Counties, 1896), I, pp. 130–68, at p.162.

14 Mackintosh, D. M., *The Irvines of Drum and their Cadet Lines 1300–1750* (Greenville, South Carolina, 1998), p. 36.

Index